נחלת שפרה
NAḤALAT SHAFRAH:
A Book of Eulogettes

HERSHEL COHEN   VICTOR M. SOLOMON

נחלת שפרה
NAḤALAT SHAFRAH:
A Book of Eulogettes

אף נחלת שפרה עלי (תהילים ט״ז:ו)
''Yea, I have a goodly heritage'' (Psalms 16:6)

HERSHEL COHEN   VICTOR M. SOLOMON

KTAV PUBLISHING HOUSE, INC.

HOBOKEN, N.J.

Library of Congress Cataloging-in-Publication Data

Cohen, Hershel, d. 1989.
  Naḥalat shafrah : a book of eulogettes / Hershel Cohen, Victor M.
Solomon.
      p.   cm.
    ISBN 0–88125–356–1
    1. Funeral sermons, Jewish.   2. Jewish sermons, American.
I. Solomon, Victor M., 1928–   . II. Title.
BM744.3.C64   1990
296.4′2—dc20
                                                  90–4455
                                                  CIP

Manufactured in the United States of America

ז״נ הא׳ הרבנית שפרה בת ר׳ יצחק
ת׳נ׳צ׳ב׳ה׳

This Volume is Lovingly Dedicated to the Memory of
Rebbetzin Shifra Cohen

ש מחה בחלקה כל ימיה

פ רשה לנצרכים ידיה

ר עיה נאמנה לצאצאיה

ה עריכה בעל נעוריה

הרבנית שפרה בת ר״ש יצחק
נפ׳ כ׳ שבט שנת תשל״ו
ת. נ. צ. ב. ה.

Acrostic poem with name of ''Shifra'' composed by her husband, Rabbi Hershel Cohen and inscribed on her monument.

To our deep sorrow, Rabbi Hershel Cohen, coauthor of this volume, was called to ישיבה של מעלה, The Academy on High, shortly after editing the galley proofs of the text.

After a long, creative life of service to his people and community, honored and loved by his family and all who knew him, he found peace and rest on January 20, 1989.

Following is the eloquent acrostic epitaph Rabbi Hershel Cohen ז״ל composed for himself.

צ ח ונעים לשונו

ב גרונו כיבד קונו

י ראת שמים במעונו

ה טיף באש אמונתו

י שב בכבוד בקהלתו

ר ועה נאמן לעדתו

ש ם טוב נחלתו

הרב צבי הירש ב״ר יוסף הכהן ז״ל

נפ׳ י״ד לחודש שבט תשמ״ט

Rabbi Hershel Cohen

ת. נ. צ. ב. ה.

ברכת אב

בהזדמנות זו אני רוצה להעניק ברכה לבתי הצנועה והמלומדת מרת צפורה לאה עם
בעלה הרב ר׳ חיים מאיר ליסטוקין שליט״א עם משפחתם הכבודה הי״ו.
לבתי המצוינת והמלומדת מאשא רבקה עם בעלה הרב דר. אביגדור מרדכי הלוי
סולומון שליט״א עם משפחתם הכבודה הי״ו.
לבני החכם והמלומד ר׳ יוסף עם רעיתו זעלדא ומשפחתם המהוללה הי״ו.
יתברכו כלם מאוצר השמים עד בלי די.
הרב צבי הירש הכהן

The publication of this book was made possible by the generosity of the following friends:

ואלה יעמדו על הברכה

BENEFACTORS

Mr. & Mrs. Arthur Dubroff	Mr. & Mrs. Murray Laulicht
Mr. & Mrs. Albert Jacob	Mr. & Mrs. William Schulder
Mr. & Mrs. Simon Jacob	Mr. & Mrs. Bruce Shoulson
Dr. & Mrs. Ira Kukin	Mr. & Mrs. Herbert Smilowitz

Mr. & Mrs. Miklos Weiss

PATRONS

Dr. & Mrs. Justin Bergman	Mr. & Mrs. Samuel Pepper
Mr. & Mrs. Herbert Blank	Mr. & Mrs. Nathan Ravin
Mr. & Mrs. Arnold Blum	Mr. & Mrs. Arthur Schwartz
Dr. & Mrs. Harold Eisenman	Dr. & Mrs. Edward Shapiro
Mr. & Mrs. Michael Jacob	Mr. & Mrs. Charles Smith
Mr. & Mrs. Murray Korman	Mr. & Mrs. Howard Weiser

SPONSORS

Anonymous	Mr. & Mrs. Joseph Finkel
Mr. & Mrs. Kurt Altman	Mr. & Mrs. Steve Flatow
Dr. & Mrs. Lawrence Batlan	Mr. & Mrs. Aaron Frank
Mr. & Mrs. Martin Beim	Mrs. Elisabeth Frank
Dr. & Dr. Stephen Bergen	Mr. & Mrs. Harold Frank
Mr. & Mrs. Berger	Mr. & Mrs. Irving Fuchs
Mr. & Mrs. Bryan Bier	Mr. & Mrs. Louis Garval
Mr. & Mrs. Horace Bier	Mrs. Carrie Geltman
Mr. & Mrs. Israel Blum	Mr. & Mrs. Ivan Gerson
Mr. & Mrs. Samuel Bornstein	Dr. & Mrs. Jerome Geyer
Mrs. Lillian Brownstein	Mr. & Mrs. David Glazer
Mr. & Mrs. Norman Cantor	Rabbi & Mrs. Anthony Glickman
Mr. & Mrs. Joel Cohen	Mr. & Mrs. David Goldberg
Dr. & Mrs. Michael Cohen	Dr. & Mrs. Herbert Goldfarb
Mr. & Mrs. Leonard Elstein	Mr. & Mrs. Richard Goldfinger
Dr. & Mrs. Herbert Ennis	Mr. & Mrs. Jay Goldfischer
Dr. & Mrs. Howard Feintuch	Dr. & Dr. Mark Grebenau
Mr. & Mrs. Max Feldman	Mr. & Mrs. George Greenfield
Mr. & Mrs. Milton Feldman	Mr. & Mrs. David Gruber

Mr. & Mrs. David Hersh
Mr. & Mrs. Abraham Hiltzik
Mr. & Mrs. Irving Hiltzik
Mr. & Mrs. Elliot Jacobs
Mr. & Mrs. S. Hirsch Jacobson
Mr. & Mrs. Lee Kahn
Mr. & Mrs. Steven Kahn
Mr. Simon Kaminetsky
Mr. & Mrs. Melvyn Kassenoff
Mr. & Mrs. Harry Katz
Dr. & Mrs. Samuel Kaye
Mr. & Mrs. Melvin-Scott Kesler
Mr. & Mrs. David Kra
Dr. & Mrs. Ethan Kra
Mr. & Mrs. Michael Krieger
Judge Stanley Levine
Rabbi & Mrs. Meyer Listokin
Dr. & Mrs. Warren Manspeizer
Rabbi & Mrs. Alvin Marcus
Mr. & Mrs. Irving Miller
Mr. & Mrs. S. Nadel
Dr. & Mrs. Bernard Neustadt
Mr. & Mrs. Irwin Novick
Mr. & Mrs. Ralph Nussbaum
Mr. & Mrs. Irving Raskin
Mr. & Mrs. Joel Rich

Mrs. Rita Rothchild
Mr. William Rothchild
Dr. & Mrs. Murray Rothman
Mr. & Mrs. Stanley Saal
Dr. and Dr. Norman Samuels
Mr. & Mrs. Herman Scherman
Dr. & Mrs. Gary Schlanger
Dr. & Mrs. Zalman Schrader
Dr. & Mrs. Bernard Schulman
Mr. & Mrs. Paul Schwartz
Mr. & Mrs. Steven Schwartz
Mr. & Mrs. Janusz Sendowski
Mr. & Mrs. Robert Silverman
Mr. & Mrs. Jack Slavitt
Rabbi Dr. & Mrs. Victor Solomon
Mr. & Mrs. Bernard Sorkin
Mr. & Mrs. Ludwig Stiefel
Mr. & Mrs. Jacob Stieger
Mrs. Gisella Strulowitz
Dr. & Mrs. Ronald Sultan
Mrs. Elizabeth Teltzer
Rabbi & Mrs. Shmuel Tokayer
Dr. & Mrs. Howard Wimmer
Mr. & Mrs. Kalman Winkler
Mr. & Mrs. Michael Witkes
Mr. & Mrs. Saul Zimmerman

Mr. & Mrs. Harold Zudick

Table of Contents

Foreword — Hershel Cohen   xxi
Introduction — Victor M. Solomon
    Hebrew   xii
    English   xxiii
Subject/Theme Topical Reference Key to Eulogettes   xiii
Tales Of My Zaydee — Yitzchak Solomon   1

Book One: Eulogettes   9

The Bow Of Light And The Bond Of Life —
    Samuel H. Solomon   11
Beyond Survival — Avraham Elchanan Solomon   13
A Woman Of Values   15
In The Company Of The Heavenly Sisterhood   17
Shepherd And Friend   19
A Eulogy In *Mezza Voce*   21
Jewish Time: Two Clocks   23
The Spiritual Dimension of Time   25
Facing Father   27
The Ultimate Measure Of Time   29
That The Tabernacle May Be Whole   31
A Mother Of Children And A Mother In Israel   33
The Loss Of A World-In-Miniature (*Olam Katan*)   35
The Root And The Fruit   37
An Arsenal Of Love   39
The Divine Garden   40
Rooted And Fruitful   42
Three Witnesses   44
Not Leaving Empty-Handed   46

The Musical Key Of Inner Conflict   47

The Blessing Of The Priest   50

Perfection From Head To Toe   52

Mourning In The Market Place   54

Too Tragic For Words   55

Unforgettable — Like An Olive Tree   57

A Celebration Of Life   59

The Vital Signs Of Life   61

The End Of Days . . . But Life Everlasting   63

Only God Can Make A Tree . . .
      But Man Must Care For it   65

Perpetual Care   67

A Global Loss   68

The Ledger And The Key   70

Moist Like Moses   72

Too Soon To Cry   74

A Fear For The Future   76

The Third Name   78

Self-Made Man   80

The New Moon Jew   82

The Sanctuary Of Public Service   84

A Woman's Place   86

In The Company Of Hashem   88

When Words Fail: Tears   90

A Different Drummer   92

A Swimming Champion: Jewish Style   94

Disagreeing Agreeably   96

With God's Approval   98

Grape Jews   100

Book Two: Unveilings   103

Tribute To A Man Of God   105

A Living Tablet   106

A Lesson In Living — From Tombstones   108
A Real Monument   110
Darkness Unto Light   112

Book Three: Divrei Torah   113

Kaddish: Consoling God   115
Reason To Believe   117

Book Four: Elegiac Sparks   119

Book Of Genesis   121
Book Of Exodus   125
Book Of Leviticus   128
Book Of Numbers   131
Book Of Deuteronomy   134

Book Five: Your Book   139

Your Eulogette Outline Forms   140
Your Evaluation and Responses   150

SUBJECT/THEME REFERENCE KEY TO EULOGETTES

(By *Sidra*, Name, Personal Characteristics and other Data)

Subject	*Page*
Aaron	31–2; 88–9
Abigail	86–7
Abraham	13–14; 59–60
Accident Victim	90–1
Aged Person	72–3
Agnostic	92–3; 96–7; 108–9
Aḥarei Mot (Sidra)	129
AIDS Victim	96–7
Alienation	117
Anonymity	82–3
Artist	63–4
Assertive Woman	86–7
Atheist	92–3; 96–7; 108–9
Authentic Person	107–8
Baal Teshuva	94–5
Bachelor	98–9
Balak (Sidra)	133
Bathsheba	15–16
Beha'alotkha (Sidra)	131
Behar (Sidra)	129
Beḥukotai (Sidra)	13–14; 130
Bemidbar (Sidra)	131
Berakhah (Sidra)	138
Bereishit (Sidra)	121
Beruriah	86–7
Beshalaḥ (Sidra)	126

Businessman, Honest   44–5; 52–3; 84–5; 100–1
Bo (*Sidra*)   125
Charitable (See *Philanthropist*)
Cheerful Person   11–12
Child   40–1; 55–6
Childless Person   33–4; 70–1; 88–9
Children, Worthy/Religious   27–8; 37–8; 42–3; 59–60
Communal Grief   68–9
Communal Leader (See *Leader*)
Creative Person   63–4
David   63–4
Deborah   33–4; 86–7
Devarim (*Sidra*)   134
Discourses at a House of Mourning (See *Divrei Torah*)
Divorcee   98–9
Divrei Torah   113–118
Doubter   92–3; 96–7
Education   106–7
Ekev (*Sidra*)   134
Elazar   88–9
Elected Public Official   84–5
Elisha Ben Avuya   92–3
Emor (*Sidra*)   129
Ethical Person   44–5; 50–1; 52–3; 54; 100–1
Faith   117
Family Tragedy   90–1
Friendship   19–20
Future Oriented   25–6
Gardener   40–1; 42–3
General Theme   112
Genuine Person   108–9
Ha'azinu (*Sidra*)   138
Hannah   86–7
Hayei Sarah (*Sidra*)   13–14; 74–5; 122
Holocaust Survivor   13–14

Homosexual 96–7
Honest Businessman (See *Businessman, Honest*)
Hope 117
House of Mourning, Talks (See *Divrei Torah*)
Hozer Biteshuvah 94–5
Hukkat (*Sidra*) 132
Hulda 86–7
Humility 21–22; 31–2; 82–3
Husband, Good 44–5
Identity, Jewish 94–5
Irreligious Person (See *Atheist*)
Isaac 59–60
Jacob 13–14; 52–3; 59–60; 63–4
Joseph 47–9; 80–1
Judah 27–8
Judge 84–5
Kaddish 115–6
Kedoshim (*Sidra*) 129
Kind Person 68–9; 100–1
Ki Tavo (*Sidra*) 137
Ki Tetzei (*Sidra*) 136
Ki Tisa (*Sidra*) 127
Kohen 31–2; 50–1
Korah (*Sidra*) 132
Lawyer 84–5
Leader 19–20; 50–1; 61–2; 86–7
Lekh Lekha (*Sidra*) 121
Longevity 72–3
Lovingkindness 96–7
Loyal Jew 65–6
Masei (*Sidra*) 133
Matot (*Sidra*) 133
Mikeitz (*Sidra*) 124
Miracles 117
Miriam 15–16; 86–7; 88–9

Mishpatim (Sidra)　　　126
Modesty (See *Humility*)
Moses　　　21–22; 63–4; 72–3; 88–9; 98–9
Musician　　　47–9; 63–4
Nashim Tzidkaniot　　　17–18; 86–7; 110–1
Naso (Sidra)　　　131
Nature Lover (See *Gardener*)
Nicknames (By Which a Person is Known)　　　78–9
Nitzavim (Sidra)　　　137
Noah　　　11–12
Noaḥ (Sidra)　　　11–12; 121
Non-Observant/Non-Practicing Person (See *Atheist*)
Old Woman　　　35–6
Optimist　　　11–12; 13–14; 25–6
Parent of Praiseworthy, Religious (See *Children, Worthy/Religious*)
Passover　　　117
Peace Loving　　　31–2; 100–1
Penitent　　　94–5
Philanthropist 15–16; 44–5; 46; 57–8; 61–2; 67–8; 82–3; 88–9;
　　　108–9; 110–1
Pinḥas (Sidra)　　　86–7; 133
Politician (See *Elected Public Official*)
Poor Person　　　70–1
Popular Person　　　61–2; 78–9
Public Servant (See *Elected Public Official*)
Rabbi　　　50–1
Rachel　　　110–1
Re'ei (Sidra)　　　135
Religious Person　　　23–4; 39; 47–9; 52–3; 65–6; 86–7
Resurrection　　　117
Righteous Woman (See *Nashim Tzidkaniot*)
Rosh Ḥodesh　　　82–3
Samuel　　　84–5
Sarah　　　35–6; 74–5
Scholar　　　63–4

Self-Made Man   80–1

Shelaḥ (Sidra)   86–7; 132

Shemini (Sidra)   128

Shemot (Sidra)   46; 125

Shiva Talks (See *Divrei Torah*)

Shofetim (Sidra)   136

Shy Person   31–2

Shimon or Simeon   98–9

Simplicity   82–3; 108–9

Single (Unmarried)   98–9

Sinner   92–3

Sisterhood President   17–18

Synthesis (Faith and Ethics)   100–1

Tazria (Sidra)   128

Talmid Ḥakham   63–4

Teacher   19–20

Tears   90–1

Terumah (Sidra)   31–2; 126

Tetzaveh (Sidra)   127

Toledot (Sidra)   123

Torah   106–7

Tragic Life   13–14

Tzav (Sidra)   128

Unexpected (Sudden) Bereavement   74–5

Untimely Death   29–30; 40–1; 55–6; 76–7

Unveiling Themes   103–112

Vaeira (Sidra)   122

Vaethanan (Sidra)   134

Vayakhel (Sidra)   127

Vayeḥi (Sidra)   52–3; 124

Vayeira (Sidra)   122

Vayeishev (Sidra)   123

Vayeitzei (Sidra)   123

Vayelekh (Sidra)   137

Vayigash (Sidra)   27–8; 124

Vayikra (Sidra) 128
Vayishlaḥ (Sidra) 13–14; 110–1; 123
Virtuous Person 70–1; 108–9
Wife Adored by Husband 35–6
Women, Pious (See *Nashim Tzidkaniot*)
Women's Organization Leader 17–18
Writer 63–4
Yeshiva Student 29–30; 40–1
Yitro (Sidra) 126
Youth 29–30; 40–1; 55–6; 76–7; 90–1

במקום הקדמה

הספר „נחלת שפרה" הוא ספר שלישי מפרי רוחי. ספרי הראשון: „ספר עזר לגירות" מדתות שונות יצא לאור בשנת 1965, ונחל שבחים נלהבים מהמבקרים. הספר השני: „סוד קיום עם ישראל" נדפס ביאפאן ובשפתם בשנת 1973, ונתפשט שם לכמה אלפים וזכה להדפסת מהדורה שמונה עשר. הספר הנוכחי הוא ספר זכרון לחותנתי שפרה ז"ל שנפטרה בלא עת. שפרה היתה אשת חיל אמיתית צנועה וחרוצה שמסרָה כל ימיה לגדל דור ישרים וי"ש. היא לקחה חבל בכמה מוסדות של תורה וצדקה, ובפרט בב"ה של בעלה חותני זצ"ל ששמשה כמזכרת במשך כמה שנים ב„עזרת הנשים" (סיסטרהוד בלע"ז) יש לקוות שהספר ימלא מקום חלל בשדה הדרוש במקצוע זה. כל רב ודרשן ימצא בו הספדים הולמים לאנשים ונשים, וגם חומר רב. הכל מוכן ומסודר בטוב טעם.

בלע המות לנצח ומחה ה׳ דמעה מעל כל פנים.

אביגדור מרדכי הלוי סולומון

Foreword

It may seem paradoxical for a *kohen* who has never entered a memorial chapel and who has never offered a eulogy at a funeral to coauthor a book of eulogies. It is true that I have not experienced the trauma of the bereaved families when the tears were flowing. However, I have shared in the grief of the family during the *shiva* days when I offered comfort drawn from the rich sources of the *Talmud* and *Midrash*. Many letters of gratitude that followed these visits testify to the value of those homilies and their significant impact on the mourners.

Shifra, to whose memory this book is dedicated, was a woman who gave so much of herself and received so little from the world. Her life revolved around me and the family as well as the *shul*, the sisterhood, and a variety of worthy institutions. Our home was always open, and *meshulochim** were frequent guests at our *Shabbos* table and also on weekdays. It is, indeed, a comfort that Shifra's memory will be enshrined in this volume, which will grace the libraries of those who knew and loved her. It is also meaningful that this book will serve as a valuable tool for rabbis in the pulpit that she valued and revered.

May these lines serve as an eminently deserved eulogy for Shifra, a life-companion of boundless love and devotion, in lieu of the eulogy that I could not deliver at the time of her funeral.

This book could not have been realized without the diligence and devotion of my esteemed and erudite son-in-law, Rabbi Dr. Victor M. Solomon. His vast knowledge in both the religious and secular fields made him a fitting co-author/editor of the book.

---

* Emissaries or collectors representing charitable institutions—or "themselves."

Moreover, his training as a clinical psychologist enabled him to compound good homiletics with sound mental health concepts. I am grateful to *Hashem* for having a co-author who is a true *talmid chacham*. May he and my other son-in-law, Rabbi Meyer Listokin, my son Joel, my daughters Zipporah Leah and Marcia Rivkah, my daughter-in-law Sally and their families continue to uphold the family tradition and thus be privileged to merit future generations of faithful Jews and fine human beings who will bring honor to us and the community.

The publication of *Naḥalat Shafra* marks the fulfillment of a very beautiful dream. It is a most pleasant occasion to express my profound thanks and sincere appreciation to my esteemed colleague and friend, Rabbi Alvin M. Marcus, spiritual leader of Congregation Ahawas Achim B'nai Jacob and David, the president Mr. Harold Frank and his officers, the chairman of the board Mr. Sam Pepper and all the board members, the president of the sisterhood Mrs. Debra Berliner, the president of the men's club, Mr. Jack Rosen and members of both groups, the chairman of adult education Dr. Edward Berliner and his committee, and all those affiliated with the *shul* for making the publication of this volume possible. No words can adequately convey my deep gratitude at this significant moment. These indescribable sentiments merely reflect my enduring appreciation for the love and esteem that were showered upon me during the years of my affiliation with this renowned congregation, and that will be forever enshrined in my heart.

May *Hashem* abundantly endow them with life's best and most precious gifts.

Hershel Cohen
20 Shevat 5748—
February 12, 1988
West Orange, New Jersey

Introduction

Bereavement is a portentious challenge familiar to clergymen, psychologists and counselors. The universal and inevitable grief experience has clearly defined ubiquitous symptoms and characteristics. There are also specific aspects and features of grief unique to the individual and his subjective encounter with tragedy. Those who minister to people's needs must familiarize themselves also with the dynamics of grief and the skills and insights necessary to render effective pastoral care to those who turn to them for help in dealing with personal loss.

Bereavement also offers a fabulous opportunity to serve fellow persons in a most benevolent and beneficial manner, at a time of anguish and existential agony. Clergymen as "Doctors of the Soul" are particularly in a strategic position to restore, revive, redeem, renew and heal the endless formations of human beings burdened with sorrow.

Three decades ago, when the subject of this book was but a fanciful notion, my call to the Philadelphia media for an open approach to death and mourning quickly became a *vox et praeteria nihil*, if not an object of derision among mourning "professionals" servicing the Jewish community. In the popular mind, sorrow was a taboo subject consigned to anonymous oblivion by a fastidious society. Since then, the theme of death, grief and mourning has attained a prominent place among matters of singular concern for individuals and communities. This may reflect a growing social sensitivity to elemental human concerns and could provide a reliable index to the humanization of people and society.

The pulpit has been a valuable and versatile vehicle in accomplishing this. In a generation, the spoken word succeeded in galvanizing communities to action in behalf of civil rights, social justice, ethical principles and religious responsibility. The pulpit has also delivered pervasive edification and sensitization in the area of grief. Moreover, the pulpit has provided a venerable and respected platform from which to reach mourners with the eulogy in time of sorrow. This medium has also demonstrated the challenge and the opportunity available to the clergyman at a time of bereavement.

There is a genuine need for a volume of brief eulogies, without elliptical prose and conceptual obfuscations, addressed to mourners' needs, suitable for adaptation and flexible for application. However, a Jewish eulogy must be more than "brief" and "consoling." In the emotionally charged and spiritually intense context of the funeral, a eulogy needs to be securely anchored in Torah and suffused with therapeutic potential. Reason dictates and wisdom prescribes a serious and skillful synthesis of religion and mental health in the service of the bereaved.

Since funerals are scheduled on short notice, the rabbi is invariably compelled to interrupt a busy, if not hectic, schedule to prepare in a twinkling a eulogy that is meaningful to the situation, a tribute to the deceased, a credit to himself and a therapeutically effective tool designed to help the mourners deal with their grief.

The practical value of a volume of brief, focused eulogies cannot be overstated. The eulogies—or better, "eulogettes"—derived from Torah, psychologically sound, linguistically correct, stylistically proper and imaginative, could be a significant resource for the busy rabbi. Handy referencing for easy accessibility and flexible application is essential, and brevity is more than a mere convenience. Convinced by our own experience and encouraged by many colleagues who expressed the need for such a volume, my father-in-law and I decided to coauthor a book of eulogettes that would meet these essential criteria.

The authors were, by virtue of training and experience, sensitive to the metaphysics of the eulogy. We were especially concerned for and attentive to the dignity of the eulogy, which has, in recent years, eroded for understandable reasons. The eulogy has been trivialized and caricatured. Many consider it irrelevant to the genuine needs of the mourners, an exercise in hypocrisy, a veritable cornucopia of unctuous flattery, adulation and grandiloquence.

As a matter of fact, the eulogy was a superb concept and continues to be a splendid means of outreach to members of the community in need of support during the most difficult time in their lives. It has great potential as a bridge-builder, converging rabbi, congregation and mourners in time of grief. Here is an opportunity to restore community solidarity and to revitalize the centrality of faith, sanctuary and community in the lives of mourners who tend to question those values when sorrow strikes.

The authors affirmed the twin rule that death does not confer sainthood on evildoers, and that atheists, agnostics and scoffers also die! They, too, deserve *honest* eulogies that *acknowledge their viewpoints without endorsing them!* The socially marginal deserve to be remembered, and AIDS victims should not be ignored. Moreover, individuals who subscribe to deviant lifestyles, while not accorded religious approval, should nonetheless be treated with respect and compassion to the fullest measure of traditional *Jewish love.*

This book has been a labor of love because it memorializes a woman of valor for whom lovingkindness was a way of life. Fiercely loyal to and supportive of her distinguished husband, she was a selfless, dedicated mother to her children—and grandchildren. Her love was unconditional and persevering. Humble and unaffected, *Rebbetzin* Shifra Cohen practiced generosity to a fault, never seeking, as I recall, personal gain or advantage. Her life was devoted to synagogue, community, friends and, especially, family.

This volume bearing her name and dedicated to her memory is but a small, though personally rewarding, tribute to a wonderful, beloved mother-in-law whom I loved as a mother and guide. ''Shifra,'' in the Torah, means ''goodness' (e.g., Psalm 16:6). Jeremiah gives it a royal connotation (Jeremiah 43:10). How fitting the congruity with our Shifra Cohen, a noble woman engaged in perpetual goodness!

May the soul of Shifra Cohen delight in this volume of *Naḥalat Shafra*, and rejoice, like Shifra of the Exodus, in the בתים, the fine Jewish homes of her children and grandchildren.

My deepest indebtedness is to my esteemed father-in-law and colleague, Rabbi Hershel Cohen, for the privilege of sharing with him in this significant work. An outstanding Talmudic scholar and pulpit rabbi who synthesizes genius and erudition, blending בקיאות and חריפות, consummate scholarship and insightful brilliance, with humility, innocence and a spontaneous sense of humor, Rabbi Hershel Cohen has been a delightful associate, a creative contributor and inspiring coauthor. All applause, acclaim and cheers belong to him, while I accept full responsibility for errors of omission and commission.

My dear wife Marcia particularly deserves more than passing words of praise and appreciation for her constant encouragement during the preparation of the manuscript, and for her insightful suggestions, helpful advice and enduring support during the many hours devoted to this book. True to the tradition bequeathed her by her mother Shifra, she patiently devoted many hours to the tedious task of editing, typing and correcting the text. She truly deserves to know how faithfully she reflects the beautiful, precious, generous virtues of her sainted mother.

My appreciation also to my sons for participating in this work:

Rabbi Samuel Halevi, for his contribution of an inspiring eulogette, "The Bow of Light and the Bond of Life;"

Shimon Yosef Levi, for his artistic and aesthetic guidance;

Yitzchak Yeranen Yaakov, for his sentimental and perceptive "Tales of My Zaydee," a tribute to his grandfather; and

Avraham Elchanan, for his brief but meaningful "sermonic spark."   עטרת זקנים בני בנים (משלי י״ז:ו׳).

Special thanks to my dear colleague and friend Rabbi Joseph I.

Singer for his sage counsel, which added an invaluable dimension to this volume.

Thanks are also due the Yeshiva University library for valuable cooperation and assistance. A cheerful librarian with an adequate support system cannot be praised enough.

Ktav Publishing House deserves countless kudos for the professionally superb and technically superior treatment accorded this project. The publisher, Mr. Bernard Scharfstein, an inexhaustible source of practical advice and encouragement, has earned my durable and cordial appreciation, as has Dr. Yaakov Elman, my very capable editor.

Finally, *todah rabbah* to Congregation Ahawas Achim B'nai Jacob and David of West Orange, New Jersey, for making the publication of this volume possible. אם אין קמח אין תורה (אבות ג':כ"א). Special thanks are due Rabbi Alvin M. Marcus, *Mora D'atra*, Harold Frank, president, and the many members of the distinguished congregation who generously launched this project as part of a tribute, honoring Rabbi Hershel Cohen for a half century of service to the congregation and community. It is, indeed, proper that in doing so they chose to celebrate and perpetuate the memory of a beloved *rebbetzin*.

Above all, I thank the Almighty for the privilege of sharing in this work. My dear father-in-law is an ideal co-author, and there is a precious sense of fulfillment in dedicating this volume to a wonderful mother-in-law, a truly life-affirming woman. בלע המות לנצח. "He will swallow up death for ever; And the Lord God will wipe away tears from off all faces . . ." (Isaiah 25:8)

And in the spirit of Shifra Cohen, of blessed memory,
"Let there be life!"

Victor M. Solomon
20 Shevat 5748—
February 8, 1988
Teaneck, New Jersey

Tales of My Zaydee

(Tribute of a Grandson)

by Yitzchak Solomon

(Zaydee is Rabbi Hershel Cohen of West Orange, New Jersey. Born in Grozov, White Russia, he studied in the *yeshivot* of Slutzk and Stuchin, Lithuania, before arriving in the United States in 1923. Formerly the spiritual leader of Congregation Ahawas Achim B'nai Jacob, one of the most prominent synagogues in Newark, New Jersey, he served there for thirty years until 1966. At present, he is Rabbi Emeritus of the merged Congregation Ahawas Achim B'nai Jacob and David in West Orange.)

Quotations from the Bible and Talmudic maxims saturate his conversation. A visit to my Zaydee, who has spent fifty-five years as a pulpit rabbi, is a very rewarding experience. On my most recent visit, I asked him why he never shared with others the story of his life in Europe and in the *yeshivot* where he spent so many of his early years in study. "I shall try," he said, "to dig out some episodes from my youthful years."

*   *   *   *   *

Until the age of twelve, I studied at my father's "small *yeshiva*" where about fifteen boys studied Talmud, Bible and Hebrew grammar. My father was one of those Talmudic scholars who did not want to be a practicing rabbi. Like others with his learning and stature, he opened a *yeshiva* as a source of income. Mother opened a bakery, and the combined income was sufficient to sustain a family of eight children.

Each student paid a fee of fifteen rubles for six months of study. The fee for Hebrew school as well as for a private tutor was always for the period of six months. This was known as a *zman*.

1

The curriculum consisted of Talmud, Bible, Prophets, history and Hebrew grammar. Father was concerned that his students should be familiar with the Hebrew language.

At the age of twelve, I left home and travelled to Slutzk, a city about twenty miles from my home. The *yeshiva* of Slutzk was famous because of its dean, the *Gaon Rav* Isser Zalman Meltzer. Boys of my age had to study for at least one year in the *mechina* class to prepare themselves for the *yeshiva*. The tests in the *mechina* were very difficult, but they were worth all the effort because it was an accomplishment to be accepted in the *Yeshiva Eitz Chayim* of Slutzk. For me, a boy from a small town, it was an exciting experience to be among the 300 young men who came to the *yeshiva* from the various cities of Russia and Poland.

Since there were no dormitories, no cafeteria and, most of all, no money, I was advised by the boys to see Dodil, a man who always had time for the boys. Dodil was in charge of finding a room for you to sleep in and *teg* (days) for meals. The best way to describe Dodil is to say that he was always running. Dodil gave me the names and addresses of five families, each of which was to provide me with two meals a day. Friday I had no *tog*, but a wealthy man gave every *yeshiva* boy five *kopekas*, which I used to buy some cookies.

I waited for *Shabbos* when I could eat with a distant cousin, rather than strangers. As for my sleeping arrangements, an aunt offered me space in the foyer of her home, where I slept on boards. With a place to sleep and five "days" arranged, I finally had peace of mind and could begin my life at the *yeshiva*.

The day at the *yeshiva* began very early with *davening*, followed by breakfast at the home of my "day" hostess. After breakfast it was back to learning until lunch, which I ate in the *yeshiva*. It consisted of some of my mother's cookies, a piece of cheese, an apple or a pear, and a glass of milk. Then it was back again to learning until the evening services. After *maariv* I went back to my "day" family for dinner.

Monday was a good *tog* because then ten of us would eat two delicious meals at the home of a wealthy Jew who then gave each boy two *kopekas* for candy. Some of the boys then went back to the *yeshiva* to learn until nine or ten o'clock, while others went to bed to be ready to get up early the next morning.

Learning in the *yeshiva* was serious business. We were not permitted to read any secular literature or even newspapers.

During my time, the *yeshiva*, which was earlier housed in a synagogue, moved into its own new building at the edge of town in an open field. The *mashgiach* was *Rav* Sheftel Kramer, the brother-in-law of *Rav* Meltzer and the father-in-law of *Rav* Ruderman, dean of the *Ner Israel Yeshiva* in Baltimore. An apartment for *Rav* Sheftel (his last name was not used) was built high above the *Beis Midrash* near the ceiling. It contained a small window through which the *mashgiach* could keep a constant, watchful eye on the boys. If you were caught *"shmoozing"* too often, you were put on the blacklist.

Rav Sheftel was not a friendly person, to say the least. Young as we were, we understood that his stern demeanor was probably due to the fact that he was blessed with five daughters. Each time he really let out his anger on us, we knew that his wife had given birth to another girl!

Horav Meltzer was not only the illustrious *rosh yeshiva* of *Eitz Chayim* in Slutzk but also the spiritual leader of the city, a community of some 12,000 people, more or less. His home was divided into two parts. One section was the residence for the *Rav*, and the other was for the *Beth Din* where the *dayanim* held court to decide on religious questions. When a problem involved money or family feuds, *Rav* Isser Zalman was invited in for consultation. The *Beth Din* room was always filled with people: *shochtim*, butchers, housewives with questionable chickens, traveling preachers and beggars. With all his responsibilities, the *Rav* had little time to involve himself with the activities of the *yeshiva*. The only time we students saw him was on Thursdays when he delivered his weekly *shiur*.

The burden of responsibility for the 300 students fell on the shoulders of the *rebbetzin*, who was superior in her own right. She was one of four daughters of Mr. Frank, a wealthy merchant in Kovno, Lithuania. He provided the best teachers for his daughters, an uncommon occurrence in those days, and they were given an extensive education in both religious and secular subjects.

A wealthy man, he was able to pick and choose husbands for his daughters, and this he did, selecting four great Talmudic giants as sons-in-law. They were: *Rav* Moshe Mordecai Epstein, *rosh yeshiva* of Slobodka and later of Hebron, Israel; *Rav* Isser Zalman of Slutzk; *Raf* Sheftel Kramer, *mashgiach* in Slutzk and later *rosh yeshiva* in New Haven, Connecticut; and *Rav* Baruch Horowitz, a prominent *Rav* in Alexot, Lithuania.

Rebbetzin Meltzer was a very gifted woman who was well versed in *Tanach* and *Midrashim*, which she quoted often to support her views. A strong disciplinarian, she was well suited for her job as secretary of the treasury of this great academy of learning.

The summer came, but there was no vacation for the boys. Learning continued twelve months a year. For a boy like me from a small town, the summer months in Slutzk were far from pleasant. There were no trees for shade and no fragrance of flowers in the air, things I remembered from home and yearned for during the long, hot days. The heat was made more unbearable because we had to wear the clothes we wore in the winter; no one had special summer clothing. It reminded me of the words of our Sages: "Go as a voluntary exile to a place of Torah" (Avoth 4:18).

Everyone wore the customary black hat. There was one boy, however, who took the liberty of putting on a straw hat. I shall always remember how we all looked at him as if he were an apostate, God forbid. This "modern" young man, *Rav* Yitzchok Shisgal, later became a *rav* on the lower East Side of New York. As the hot summer days wore on, I longed more and more for home to see my parents and taste Mother's cooking and the fresh fruits that grew in abundance near our house. The "three weeks" and *Tish B'av*, a time of sadness and mourning at the *yeshiva*, had come and gone, so I decided to go home for *Shabbat Nachamu* to refresh myself. The only problem was transportation expenses, which amounted to thirty-five *kopekas*. I went to the *rebbetzin* and told her of my desire to visit my home and asked her for the money. She looked me over and said: "A young, healthy boy like you can walk to Grozov." I walked away from her with a bitter taste in my mouth, which I remember to this day.

We all had to yield to the whims of the *rebbetzin*, since she had dominion over the treasury. This control led to a great embarrassment for her. One day we were all informed that no one would get his monthly allowance because there was a shortage of money. Everyone was very secretive about the reason for the shortage, but finally the mystery was solved. Somehow, the money was mysteriously lost by the *rebbetzin* and no one wanted to talk about the circumstances of the loss.

The word *ilui* is a very popular term at all *yeshivot*. It is synonymous with an individual who has a photographic memory. There are many great *rabbonim*, but there are very few *iluyim*.

While most *rabbonim* achieve their knowledge due to the long hours of study, the *iluyim* are given the Torah on a silver platter. The gates of Torah are wide open to them. We had many outstanding *talmidim* in Slutzk. Among them were Dovid of Bookie, *Rav* Kaganoff, who was a *rosh yeshiva*, in Chicago, and Moshe Aaron of Timkowitz, *Rav* Polayef, a *rosh yeshiva* at R.I.E.T.S. Brilliant as they were, however, they were not considered *iluyim*. Imagine our excitement then, when a young man in his early twenties walked into the *yeshiva* one day accompanied by Kaganoff and Polayef, who introduced him as the *ilui* of Sislowitz. We were told that this slim, young man would treat us to a *d'var Torah*. The *d'var Torah* lasted two and a half hours, and it consisted of an analytical *shiur* dealing with *halachah* on the highest level in form and content. He spoke rapidly and appeared very relaxed. This timid *bochur* became quite well known. His name was *Hagaon* Aaron Kotler of Lakewood.

It was not long afterward that *Hagaon* Kotler became the

choson of *Horav* Meltzer's daughter, and I witnessed one of the most impressive weddings that any *rav* or *yeshiva* boy was ever privileged to see. It was talked about for weeks afterward. *Horav* Henkin, the *gaon* and *posek*, once remarked that the *drasha* that *Horav* Kotler delivered at the *Tnoyim*, even he or *Rav* Isser Zalman could match; but the *drasha* that *Rav* Aaron gave at the wedding dinner, neither he nor *Rav* Aaron's father-in-law could duplicate.

After four years at the *yeshiva* of Slutzk I decided to go to another *yeshiva* to learn. The one I chose was farther from home, a *yeshiva* in Stuchin near Vilna. A day after *Pesach* I prepared myself for the long journey. It was the first time in my life that I traveled on a train. I felt very much at home in this town with its quiet streets and friendly people. I felt the atmosphere would be very conducive for study.

There were no *teg* (days) in Stuchin. A committee from the town welcomed every new student and gave him an address where he would be lodged and an address where he would eat on *Shabbos*. I noticed that the committee was looking me over.

Rav Leib Chasman, *rav* of Stuchin and founder of the *yeshiva*, was a disciple of the famous *Rav* Israel Salanter, the founder of the *Mussar* movement, so lectures on *mussar* were an important part of the curriculum in Stuchin. Every *Shabbos* between *mincha* and *maariv*, *Rav* Leib would set aside time for a short lecture on *mussar*, which left a deep impression on me to this day.

Hagaon Rav Alter Shmulewitz, Dean of the *yeshiva*, was a dynamic person with an angelic face. He was, however, somewhat disorganized. One day he walked into *shul* with only one shoe on. One of the boys quickly ran to his home to bring him his other shoe. The typical absentminded professor! While *Rav* Leib was very reserved and spoke slowly like a British diplomat, *Rav* Alter was very *heimish* and friendly with the boys. His *shiurim* were deep like those of *Rav* Kotler, and very logical. Here my learning flourished. Unlike Slutzk, where the *yeshiva* boy was not treated with great respect, the people in Stuchin held the student in high esteem. The pure Torah air of Vilna reached out and permeated the town near it, and we felt a warmth in Stuchin from people the likes of which I have never met elsewhere in my lifetime.

Looking back at the years I spent in those two *yeshivot*, I am happy that my formative years were molded by such great *gaonim* as *Rav* Meltzer, *Rav* Shmulewitz and *Rav* Leib Chasman, whose *mussar* sermonettes were my guidelines for a moral and ethical life.

I give thanks to *Hashem* for the privilege of faithfully serving Him and my fellow Jews for over fifty years. I have been most fortunate to see my children, grandchildren and great-grandchildren walking in the path of Torah and mitzvot. May the words of the Prophet be truly realized in my family: "My spirit which shall be upon you and my words which I have put in your mouth shall not depart from your mouth, nor from the mouth of your children, nor from the mouth of your children's children, says the Lord, henceforth and forever" (Isaiah 59:21).

(Originally published as a two-part series in *Hamevaser, Student Publication of Traditional Thought and Ideas*, The Jewish Studies Divisions of Yeshiva University Publication, on March 14, 1984 and April 12, 1984.)

Book One

EULOGETTES

ברוחו שמים שפרה (איוב כ"ו: י"ג)
''By His breath the heavens are serene'' (Job 26:13)

"The Bow of Light and the Bond of Life"

A Tribute to His Grandmother's Memory

by Rabbi Samuel H. Solomon

(For a person who had a cheerful outlook on life; an optimist;
a man named Noah; *sidrah Noah*)

את קשתי נתתי בענן והיתה לאות ברית ביני ובין הארץ (בראשית ט:י"ג). ''I have
set my bow in the cloud, and it shall be a token of a covenant
between Me and the earth'' (Genesis 9:13).

The rainbow betokens a covenant of life between *Hashem* and
the *earth*. It is an affirmation of life, a binding assurance that
heaven and earth are not dichotomous. A rainbow is pledged to
articulate and conjoin the two realms, proclaiming the entelechy
of life even as it proceeds to implant itself in the earth.

What is a rainbow? By definition, a rainbow is a circle or, from
the usual viewpoint, an arc of a circle, exhibiting in concentric
bands the colors of the spectrum, and formed opposite the sun by
the refraction and reflection of the sun's rays in drops of rain. Our
Sages compare Torah to water, *mayim hayim*, living water, or
water of life. Water is a simple, ubiquitous, familiar substance,
without which all life would cease. Yet, contained in each tiny
drop in the mist is a kaleidoscope of the colors of life's spectrum.
Like a prism, water will display the dazzling multicolored
arrangement from the sun's light, as Torah reflects the spectrum
of life itself.

However, to perceive the polychromatic display, one must
view the rainbow from the right perspective. Two people can look
at a rainbow: one sees a beautiful, inspiring spectral phenomenon
and the other does not. The vapor and the sunlight are there, but
only the eye of the beholder can determine the effect.

So it is with life and death. God says that the sign of His relationship with man and mankind is the rainbow, which symbolizes an eternal covenantal bond. Man's awareness of this sign is not forced upon him. He must search for it in the darkest hour of tragedy as he strains to hear the faint footsteps of the Redeemer, to perceive the barest silhouette of God's presence in his anguished moment of bereavement.

Judaism is realistic. It does not say that this is easy. Life's meaning is determined by a perception; the angle of the viewer differentiates the believer from the perplexed. The light is always there, but the faculty of sight—better yet, a spiritual quantum of insight—must be employed to perceive it. *Hashem's* presence, like the rainbow, can bridge the lugubrious grave in the bowels of the earth with the joyous promise of heavenly hope, and secure the צרור החיים, the eternal bond of life that unites the dead with the living and invalidates death.

The Talmud relates that the World to Come, the realm beyond the rainbow, is suffused with a sacred primeval light from early Genesis, which God prudently reserved for the *tzadikim*, the righteous in the World to Come (Hagigah, 12a). We pray that __________ __________ be among those *tzadikim vetzidkoniot* who may bask in that celestial light.

May her lustrous memory be a constant blessing to her beloved family to dispel the shadow of grief and reveal to the perceptive mourner the צרור החיים, the bond of life.

תהא נשמתה צרורה בצרור החיים.

May the soul of __________ __________ be bound up in the bond of eternal life. Amen.

"*Beyond Survival*"

Tribute to the memory of a Bubby

by Avraham Elchanan Solomon

(For one who has experienced a difficult life, with tragedies; a Holocaust survivor; an optimist; one named Abraham or Jacob; for *sidrot Ḥayei Sarah*, *Vayishlaḥ* and *Beḥukotai*)

ויקם אברהם מעל פני מתו (בראשית כ״ג:ג) "And Abraham rose up from before his dead" (Genesis 23:18).

The passing away of Sarah his wife had been the most tragic experience in Abraham's life. This saintly woman with whom he had walked before *Hashem*, served his fellowmen, and raised a son, Isaac, who was destined to become a giant step toward the fulfillment of the great divine promise, was no longer among the living.

How does a spiritual giant like Abraham deal with tragedy? One would certainly expect him to survive. But is *survival* all that could be expected of a saintly person like Abraham?

His grandson Jacob also experienced many tragedies in his painful life. He had to flee his brother Esau and abandon his parental home. He was enslaved to a greedy Laban for many years. His daughter Dinah was violated by Shechem, which set off a tragic series of events. Yet, the Torah relates: ויבא יעקב שלם עיר שכם (בראשית ל״ג:י״ח), "and Jacob came in peace to the city of Shechem," (Genesis 33:18), which Rashi interprets: *Shalem begufo . . . shalem bemamono . . . shalem betorato*—physically, financially and spiritually intact. In other words, Jacob not only *survived his ordeals; he was actually refined and perfected by them. Thus, the laws of* ערכין, human valuation, *follow* the תוכחה, catalogue of suffering and retribution. It is as though the Torah expects a person to grow and prosper in and through tragedy.

The Holocaust would have destroyed a lesser nation. In fact, some Jews did abandon their Judaism in despair. But the true survivors not only survived, they ensured the continuity and imperishability of the Jewish people by securing the State of Israel, which they anchored in the Holocaust *ḥurban*, and by building great Torah institutions throughout the world.

Abraham also went beyond survival. ויקם אברהם מעל פני מתו. And Abraham *rose up* from before his dead. When his wife Sarah passed away, Abraham was not defeated. In fact, ויקם אברהם Abraham was *elevated* by the tragic experience, and then went on with the business of life and *mitzvot*.

My Bubby was a very special person. I do not remember her as she played with me and fussed over me. However, I could sense her presence long after she was gone, and can still experience her beautiful heritage of Torah and *mitzvot* which she left for me to carry on. The tragedy of her passing could not silence her instructions to an upcoming generation. The Torah lifestyle and the spiritual elevation she has left with us continue to inspire and grow.

It reminds me of Bubby's classic bookmark, which she herself crocheted. The helter-skelter of stitching made no sense until I discovered that I was looking at the wrong side of the bookmark. When I turned it over, the mystery was resolved. There was the clearly spelled out passage from the 23rd Psalm: ה' רועי לא אחסר, "The Lord is my shepherd, I shall not want!"

"A Woman of Values"

ז"נ אחותי הא׳ גאלדה אסתר בת ר׳ אברהם אלחנן הלוי ת׳נ׳צ׳ב׳ה׳
Dedicated to the memory of my beloved sister Goldie Moses

by Victor M. Solomon

(For a woman devoted to congregational and communal causes and educational institutions)

ר׳ יוסי בר׳ יהודה אומר שלשה פרנסים טובים עמדו לישראל. אלו הן: משה ואהרון ומרים; וג׳ מתנות טובות ניתנו על ידם, ואלו הן: באר וענן ומן. באר בזכות מרים . . . מתה מרים נסתלק הבאר שנאמר: „ותמת שם מרים" וכתיב בתריה: „ולא היה מים לעדה" (במדבר כ׳); וחזרה בזכות שניהם (תענית ט.)

The earth's land surface is only one-sixth that occupied by the seas. Yet, when man needs to drink water, he must seek the pure, precious liquid in wells dug deep into the bowels of the earth, because ocean water is salty and unfit for human consumption.

Six hundred thousand Israelites left Egypt with Moses and wandered throughout the Sinai Wilderness for forty years, but only one person, a woman, could provide pure water for her people, and their thirst was quenched in her *zechut*, due to her merit. Miriam, as a young girl, displayed a deep sense of compassion when she stood at the Nile eagerly looking after the reed basket to see what would happen to her baby brother. The excellence of the water given to her desert people in her *zechut* was matched only by the purity of her young compassionate heart.

________ __________, whom we mourn today, was a veritable Miriam. Her life of concern and caring for others reflected nobly the ancient Jewish values of love and responsibility for our fellowman epitomized in the life of her ancestress Miriam. She offered charity to the needy, clothing to the orphaned, shelter to the homeless and her heart—herself—to the troubled and afflicted. Active in behalf of every charitable institution in the community, she found adequate time for her children whom she mothered in the most beautiful, spiritually ennobling way. And her husband and children reciprocated with love, admiration and respect.

The *Eishet Chayil,* which King Solomon dedicated to his own mother, Bathsheba, is an accurate description of ___________ ___________ and a fitting tribute to her blessed memory. And her reward is lovingly outlined in this touching 31st chapter of Proverbs: "Dignity and honor are her garb and she smiles looking at the future" (Proverbs 31:10).

The painful and tragic bereavement to the family of ___________ ___________ is compounded by the irreparable loss to the entire community. She will be missed by all who were sustained and nourished by her compassion, and whose desperate thirst for human kindness was quenched at the spring of refreshing, lifegiving pure water drawn through the *zechut* of ___________ ___________, a pure and giving soul.

שלום לעפרה

"In the Company of the Heavenly Sisterhood"

ז״נ אמי מורתי הא׳ טילה רבקה בת ר׳ יעקב ת׳נ׳צ׳ב׳ה׳

Dedicated to the memory of my beloved mother,
Tillie R. Solomon

by Victor M. Solomon

(For a woman active in the synagogue and Jewish communal
life who lived an exemplary life)

‏בזכות נשים צדקניות שבאותו הדור נגאלו אבותינו ממצרים (סוטה י״א.)‏ "In the merit of the righteous women of that generation, our ancestors were redeemed from Egypt" (Sotah, 11a).

In every generation eminent Jewish women left a memorable imprint on Jewish history. The "righteous women" of Egypt were the ones whose meritorious achievements brought redemption. Their courage and faith in the ultimate triumph of freedom healed the sagging spirits of their enslaved husbands and inspired countless generations of oppressed Jews and the downtrodden of all nations.

The Israelite woman's boundless faith in a mericful God and her staunch defense of Jewish religious values often saved the fledgling Jewish nation in critical moments in history. It was the Jewish woman, according to Rabbinic tradition, who courageously refused to partake in the Golden Calf apostacy. When the scouts/spies returned to Moses with a discouraging, albeit majority, report concerning the Promised Land, not one woman in Israel joined the ill-fated rebellion against *Hashem*. In fact, the women were exempted from the decree that the *dor hamidbar*, the erstwhile slave generation, perish in the wilderness, and many of them were privileged to enter the Promised Land! Nachmanides points out that the women set a noble example of dedication in the erection of the Sanctuary.

We are assembled here today for a sad but historic event; to bid farewell to a prototypical woman whose life was a faithful reflection of the Miriams, Deborahs, Abigails and Esthers, and the countless *nashim tzidkaniot*, those righteous unsung spiritual heroines who illumined our glorious history. _____________ _____________ served as sisterhood president, AMIT Women president, and Hadassah president. More, she kept a kosher kitchen, lived an ethical and moral lifestyle and provided a genuine Jewish home for her wonderful family.

Today, she joins the ranks of the *nashim tzidkaniot* in Heaven to continue her prayers in behalf of Israel and her family, in the company of that immortal Sisterhood *shel maalah*, and in the presence of the merciful God she loved and served.

שלום לעפרה

"Shepherd and Friend"

ז"נ הרה"ג ר' ירוחם פישל אריה ב"ר אשר ת'נ'צ'ב'ה'
Dedicated to the memory of my esteemed colleague and friend
Rabbi Philip L. Rabinowitz

by Victor M. Solomon

(For a good friend, a devoted teacher or communal leader)

(תהילים כג,א) מזמור לדוד ה' רועי לא אחסר "The Lord is my shepherd I shall not want" (Psalms 23:1).

For generations, Psalm 23 has been the most familiar scriptural reading at funerals and memorial meetings for Jews and other faith communities alike.

One is inclined to wonder why the Psalmist compares the Lord to a shepherd instead of, let us say, a father or mother, or some other significant person with noble and sentimental connotations and denotations.

The reason, incredible at first blush, is the fact, often featured in newspaper stories, that even father and mother may be—and frequently are—neglectful of their children. In such instances, the court assumes responsibility for the child and makes the youngster a ward of the state.

The shepherd, however, remains constantly and unflinchingly watchful over his four-legged charges. He entertains them with the flute, drives away preying beasts and leads them to greener pastures and refreshing spring waters. His sole vocation is tending to the safety and welfare of his flock. The linguistic connection between רוֹעֶה, shepherd, and רֵעַ, friend or colleague, is more than coincidental; a good shepherd is also a devoted friend.

_________ _________ is best described as both a good shepherd and a devoted friend. His dedication to the children entrusted to him for their intellectual nurture and training reflected the finest qualities of the teacher prescribed by our tradition. Indeed, he was more than a vigilant shepherd or teacher; he was a devoted friend to his students as well as to their parents.

His passing is a shocking loss not only to those who learned Torah at his feet, but a tragedy for the Jewish community and to the cause of Jewish education to which he consecrated his very life and his formidable skill as an educator. ____________ ____________ was a worthy רוֹעֶה and a wonderful רֵעַ.

May the memory of ____________ ____________ always rekindle pleasant memories worthy of emulation.

שלום לעפרו

"A Eulogy in Mezza Voce"

(For a person whose humility was not corrupted by wealth
and power)

כי נח נפשיה דרב הונא סבור לאתובי ספר תורה אפורייהו. אמר להו רב חיסדא: מלתא
דבחייה לא סבירא ליה, השתא ליקום ליעבר ליה? (מועד קטן, כה.) "When the
soul of Rav Huna came to repose, they thought of placing a scroll
of the Torah on his bier. Said Rav Ḥisda to them: Should one do
for him now something that he did not countenance in his lifetime?"

When the great sage *Rav* Huna passed away, his friends
wished to place a Torah scroll on his bier, or hearse, as was the
custom with deceased kings and sages (e.g., King Hezekiah, cf
Bava Kamma, 17b). However, *Rav* Ḥisda advised against it,
recalling that *Rav* Huna had, himself, opposed the practice of
placing Torah scrolls on biers of the deceased.

______________ ___________ often expressed dissatisfaction with
contemporary eulogies in America, which tend to exaggerate the
virtues of individuals who are neither great themselves nor prac-
titioners of greatness in behalf of others. I trust that this eulogy
will conform with the high standard of honesty he has bequeathed
to us.

______________ ____________, though a person of means, eschewed
the amenities and honors usually bestowed upon the wealthy.
Steeped in wisdom and culture, both sacred and secular, and more
than qualified for high office in any civic or communal institution,
he never coveted power or privilege derived from formal public
leadership. But in his personal life and in his interpersonal rela-
tionships, he nobly reflected the three ideal attributes of our
people: רחמנים, בישנים וגומלי חסדים, compassion, modesty and the
practice of lovingkindness—for he was a true son of our patriarchs
who modeled these sublime characteristics.

Candor and propriety would have dictated an impressive catalogue of ______________ ______________'s virtues, qualities and accomplishments—but it would not have pleased him. ______________ ______________, like *Rav* Ḥisda, did not believe in placing a Torah scroll on the bier of the deceased. The highest praise ______________ ______________ could be persuaded to accept in the framework of a eulogy is that he was a humble and honest man—the highest compliment bestowed by the Torah upon משה רבנו, our teacher, Moses.

May the memory of ______________ ______________ be a blessing to his dear family and to us all.

שלום לעפרו

"*Jewish Time: Two Clocks*"

(For a religious person devoted to the synagogue and other
Jewish institutions)

When the celebrated saint and defender of Jews, Rabbi Levi
Yitzchak of Berditchev, so the story goes, felt that his days were
numbered, he assembled his family and friends, and said: "When
the clock in the house and the clock in the synagogue stop, you
will know that I am no longer among the living!"

Rabbi Levi Yitzchak's message to his loved ones was patently
clear. When a person leaves this world, activities cease, accomplishments stop, deeds are no longer done, and his life comes to an
abrupt halt. His personal clock has been stilled. But there is
another clock that can go on ticking. The "shul clock" need not
stop, for it can continue functioning to measure the fruits of his
life's work in behalf of an eternal God and His undying people.

We often note with chagrin compounded by utter frustration
the passing of people who leave no void in the community
because they contributed nothing or very little during their lifetime to the spiritual enrichment of their people and the preserva-
tion of their religious and cultural heritage. When their private
clock stops, so does the timepiece in the synagogue.

_______________ _____________, whom we mourn today, was a noble
soul whose life was guided by two clocks. His home was a truly
Jewish fortress in which the *mitzvot* and values of Judaism were
religiously observed. But his dedication to his Jewish faith was not
confined to the home. The clock in his home was synchronized
with the "shul clock," which set the pace and by whose rhythm
he walked through life. To the synagogue he offered his time and
means. He graciously supported *yeshivot* and Torah causes as
well as every Jewish institution, from orphan homes to Jewish
National Fund, that turned to him for assistance.

At this very moment, as this eulogy is being offered, his clock in the synagogue is still ticking and telling time, and celebrating, not the demise, but the *life* of _____________ _____________ and his good deeds.

You, his children, whom he loved and to whom he bequeathed a beautiful and undying heritage, will also celebrate his life as you continue to tell time from your father's "shul clock," and teach your children and their children to guide their lives by that enduring and precise chronometer.

שלום לעפרו

"The Spiritual Dimension of Time"

(For a person who sanctified his life in the present because he
valued the verdict of futurity).

„אמר לי תא אחלי לך היכא דנשקי ארעא ורקיע אהדדי. שקלתא לסילתאי אתנחתא
בכוותא דרקיעא. אדמצלינא בעיתיה ולא אשכחיתה. אמינא ליה איכא גנבי הכא? אמר
לי האי גלגלא דרקיעא והוא דהדר נטר עד למחר הבא ומשכחת לה׳" (בבא בתרא ע״ד.).

The Talmud relates a fascinating story about the Jewish
Aesop, Rabbah bar Bar Chanah. A Bedouin once invited the Sage
to the point of junction between heaven and earth. At the place of
symphysis, the Sage placed his basket on a window sill and said
his prayers. Later, when he was about to leave, he could not find
his basket. "Are there any thieves in Heaven?" he asked. "No,"
was the answer, "but everything here is rotating. Tomorrow at
this time you will find your basket in the same place where you
left it." (Baba Bathra, 74a).

Modern society with its Madison Avenue mentality has dedicated special days, weeks and months of commemoration
throughout the calendar year. There are Mother's and Father's
Days, Stamp Collector's Week, and Health, Heart and Book
Months. All of them designate and celebrate "today" studiously,
frivolous and oblivious about the future. There are no
"tomorrow"-days.

In the spiritual configuration of time, the past is a vital reposi-
tory of redemptive history and precious traditions. The present
plays a decisive role as the context in which normative religious
practice, ethical behavior and ritual observance are accomplished.
However, there is also the future, which occupies a significant
place in the spiritual taxonomy of time. In this tabulation, there is
no substitute for patience. One must wait with forbearance, like
Rabbah bar Chanah, for the next day and the systematic action of
natural forces to run their predictable course.

_____________ _____________, whom we eulogize today, was one of those rare individuals who do not live only in the convenient past or ensconce themselves in a comfortable present. _____________ _____________ hyphenated heaven and earth during his lifetime and suffused the mundane with time-transcendent spiritual meaning, infusing earthly concerns with heavenly values.

He prepared for himself an attributal tomorrow that will be an enduring memorial to a person who lived in the spiritual dimension of time. May we mourn less and emulate more the quintessence of _____________ _____________'s affirmative view of life.

שלום לעפרו

"Facing Father"

(For a man named Judah; a person whose children will remain devoted Jews; for the *Sidra Vayigash*. Challenging children to remain religious.)

כי איך אעלה אל אבי והנער איננו אתי פן אראה ברע אשר ימצא את אבי. (בראשית מד:לד) "For how shall I go up to my father, if the lad be not with me? Lest I look upon the evil that shall come on my father" (Genesis 44:34).

Judah, who assumed full responsibility for Benjamin's safety, could not reconcile himself to facing his father without the lad. His respect for his father and his reverence for the venerable patriarch precluded the possibility of compounding his grief.

Every father is duty bound to bring his child close to the Heavenly Father, i.e., to rear him in a manner that will bring joy and blessing to God and man. If this obligation is binding and compelling during a person's lifetime, how much more so after the parents are called to their heavenly rest. It is a Jewish categorical imperative that children remain faithful to the spiritual heritage of their parents.

Every one of us will come, one day, before our Father in Heaven, some of us, sadly, without the *na'ar*, the lad. While father (mother) was alive, he (she) presided over a fine traditional Jewish home. When he (she) was summoned by the Creator, all the surrepetitious erosion of acculturation and assimilation became evident, for the *na'ar*, the lad, or better the *no'ar*, the youth, was not there to carry on in the traditions of the father (mother). Children often abandon their father's (mother's) heritage precisely at this critical moment, when Jewish continuity is at stake, when the issue of Jewish survival is decided.

It is comforting, even in this climate of mourning, to observe the sincere determination of children to remain true to their

father's (mother's) traditions. And this is the greatest tribute and
the most eloquent eulogy for a devoted Jew: father (mother) will
not appear before his (her) Maker empty-handed. He (she) will
face his (her) Heavenly Father with the assurance that the *na'ar*,
their children, like Benjamin, are not lost to Judaism, that they
remain staunchly loyal and unyieldingly devoted to the Torah
concepts and precepts that they learned at home.

_______________ _______________ is coming home to *his* (*her*) Father
with the excellent credentials of a successful father (mother) who
has done well by his (her) children and fulfilled his (her) mission
of a good father (mother) in Israel. He (she) has imbued his (her)
children with a Jewish sense of duty and a genuine devotion to the
Jewish faith. He (she) comes to his (her) Father והנער עמו, proud
and happy that what he (she) treasured most during his (her) lifetime will be upheld by his (her) children who will continue in the
path of the generations.

שלום לעפרו

"The Ultimate Measure of Life"

ז״נ הרה״ג ר׳ צבי ב״ר אברהם יצחק ת׳נ׳צ׳ב׳ה׳
Dedicated to the memory of my dear brother-in-law
Rabbi Harold Fefferman

by Victor M. Solomon

(For a young Torah student who died in his prime)

כד דמיך ר׳ בון בר ר׳ חייא על ר׳ צעירא ואפטר. עלוי ״מתוקה שנת העובד אם מעט
ואם הרבה יאכל והשבע לעשיר איננו מניח לו לישון״ (קהלת ה: י״א) אין כתיב כאן
אלא „אם מעט אם הרבה יאכל״ . . . יגע זה בתורה לעשרים ושמונה שנה. (ירושלמי,
ברכות פ״ב:ח) ''Rabbi Bun the son of Rabbi Ḥiyya went to Rabbi
Zeira and died. (He was eulogized) concerning him: 'Sweet is the
sleep of the laboring man, whether he eat little or much; but the
satiety of the rich will not suffer him to sleep.' (Ecclesiastes 5:11).
This one (R. Bun) strove in the Torah in twenty-eight years (more
than) a diligent student could study in a hundred years.'' (Jerusalem Talmud, Berachot 2:8)

The most agonizing tragedy is the death of a young person,
the early termination of a precious life before the full measure of
years could bring fulfillment of dreams, attainment of ideals,
achievement of goals.

Rabbi Zeira expressed the sentiments of many of us today
when he eulogized the twenty-eight-year-old Rabbi Bun, the son
of Rabbi Ḥiyya. In a tragedy of this genre and magnitude, consolation can be found only in the belief that the quality of life lived
more than compensates for quantity of years lost; that achievement and meaning in life are attained not through the arithmetic
of the calendar but by the singular criteria of Torah and *Halachah*.
_______________ _____________ devoted his all too brief life to study
of Torah. The *yeshiva* was his home. There he combined days and

nights in diligent pursuit of genuine Torah scholarship. Both teachers and peers loved and respected him, and during his brief tenure on earth he amassed a vast amalgam of Judaica from a variety of sources and on every level of erudition that would be the envy of seasoned scholars. "How sweet is his rest among the righteous and pious." His memory has earned an everlasting place of honor within the *yeshiva* walls, and his name will always be remembered lovingly by his colleagues, with respect and admiration. For, in the final audit, it will be found that __________ __________ lived his tragically short life not in the realm of quantifiable time but in the context of noble achievement as a student and practitioner of spiritual values.

May his father, mother and family derive consolation from the awareness that they, like our Patriarch Abraham, have offered their precious son on *Har Hamoriah*, the place of *Hora'a*, the sacred institution where he consecrated the best years of his life to Torah study and the observance of *mitzvot*. There can be no greater tribute to any person with an awareness of the *tzelem Elokim*, the Divine Image.

שלום לעפרו

"That the Tabernacle May be Whole"

(For a humble, unassuming, modest, shy, soft-spoken, peace-loving person; a man named Aaron; a *kohen*; *Sidra Terumah*).

The *Yalkut* relates that when the Tabernacle was completed, Moses gave the people a full financial accounting of the construction costs. He was amazed to discover that he was 1,775 *sh'kalim* short. Moses became very anxious because he feared that the people would accuse him of embezzlement. At that very moment *Hashem* opened his eyes and he beheld the *krasim* (clasps). Moses immediately realized that the missing money had been spent on the clasps.

We are always ready to admire the exotic. The unusual catches our eye, but we neglect to appreciate the ordinary, the things that surround us daily. Moses surely was proud when he saw the various sacred objects displayed. There was the Ark, the *menorah*, the altar. He failed, however, to notice the tiny *krasim*, although these clasps were greatly responsible for making the Tabernacle a "whole one," as we read: "And thou shalt make fifty clasps of gold and couple the curtains one to another with the clasps that the Tabernacle may be one whole" (Exodus 26:6).

A synagogue is a Sanctuary in miniature. There are members who symbolize the Ark. They devote time to the study of Torah or support students of Torah. There are others who are like the altar, offering their time and energy for the benefit of the *shul*. There are also those who are like the *menorah*, seeing to it that the Sanctuary is bright and comfortable. However, there are those members who, by their very nature, do not promulgate their activities in behalf of the *shul*. They do their sacred work with no fanfare or publicity. These members are the *krasim* of our synagogue.

_____________ _____________ was a humble man, modest, soft-spoken and shy. He was also a doer, who worked for worthy

causes quietly and without fanfare. He was one of the *krasim*, the
"golden clasp" of our congregation who, in his unassuming, quiet
way, had a good word for everyone and by example made our
Tabernacle a "whole one." He was of the disciples of Aaron, אוהב
שלום ורודף שלום, "loving peace and pursuing peace, loving thy
fellow-creatures, and drawing them near to the Torah" (Avoth
1:12).

Alas, too few *krasim* Jews remain, which makes the passing of
__________ __________ so much more painful and frightening.
Yet, the good he has done, the hearts he has won and the souls he
has touched will inspire a new generation of *krasim* Jews who will
follow in his footsteps, to build bridges between people and to
become the "clasps" that will, in this era of pluralistic disintegra-
tion, hold our community together "that the Tabernacle may be
one whole."

שלום לעפרו

"A Mother of Children and a Mother in Israel"

לז״נ אחותי צפורה לאה בת ר׳ יוסף הכהן ע״ה שנפטרה ערורית.

Dedicated to the memory of my beloved sister

by Hershel Cohen

(For a woman who was childless but devoted her life to orphans, students and child-related causes; a woman named Deborah).

The Torah lists two kinds of mothers. There is the אם הבנים שמחה, "a joyful mother of children" (Psalms 113:9) and the אם בישראל "mother in Israel" (Judges 5:7). The "joyful mother of children" of the psalmist finds great personal satisfaction in the blessings of motherhood. The "mother in Israel" personified by the prophetess Deborah gives of herself so that those who have no mother will not be motherless.

The biblical Deborah was a genuine mother in Israel who nurtured and protected a people orphaned by persecution and war. "עד שקמתי דבורה שקמתי אם בישראל„ "until that I Deborah arose, that I arose a mother in Israel" (Ibid). Countless mothers who left large families are vaguely remembered beyond the family circle. Not so with Deborah, whose name is enshrined in Scripture; she exerted a vital influence in the history of our people. Throughout the generations she has been a symbol of courage and heroism, the classic ideal mother. A woman of such grace and virtue was often compared to Deborah who transcended a mere mother of children; she was the noble "mother in Israel."

___________ ___________, whom we mourn today, was a genuine אם בישראל, a "mother in Israel." Her devotion to students of Torah and orphans of all ages, including those in the Home for the Aged, will serve as an everlasting monument to her selflessness in the community. Her name, like that of Deborah, the biblical "mother in Israel," will be enshrined in the hearts of the children she mothered and the many orphans of all ages for whom she was a true "mother in Israel."

תהא נשמתה צרורה בצרור החיים

May her soul be bound up in the bond of the living, and her name continue to be a blessing among those who loved her.

"*The Loss of a World-in-Miniature (Olam Katan)*"

ז״נ הא׳ חיה בת ר׳ מרדכי ת׳נ׳צ׳ב׳ה׳

Dedicated to the memory of my dear cousin Anna Balaban

by Victor M. Solomon

(For a noble old woman who was honored and loved by her husband)

"ויבא אברהם לספד לשרה ולבכתה (בראשית, כ״ג,ב׳). And Abraham proceeded to mourn for Sarah and to bewail her" (Genesis 23:2).

Shortly before Sarah's death, two infamous cities, Sodom and Gomorrah, were incinerated, and their wicked inhabitants obliterated by the wrath of God. One may wonder, with a reasonable margin of justification, at the propriety of Abraham's grief when Sarah, an old, 127-year-old woman, passed away, against the background of that double disaster in which thousands had lost their lives.

Upon reflection, one is inclined to perceive in this anomaly a vital Jewish concept, the belief in human sanctity. The death of an individual human being is infinitely more painful than the loss of a city. The Torah, at the very beginning of time, proclaimed what was later known as the *imago dei*, that a human being is created in the divine image, and that the death of one person is the loss of a segment of God's reflection. The family is bereaved, that is, robbed of a significant person, but there is also a theological tragedy, the disappearance of a precious part of the Creator.

At a time when the smoke was still rising from the smoldering funeral pyres of Sodom and Gomorrah, the discreet and benevolent Abraham, undistracted by the background havoc, devoted himself to the grief and eulogy for his beloved wife Sarah, because his own "world-in-miniature" was in ruins, destroyed by the death of his beloved wife.

The passing of ___________ ___________ is to her bereaved husband and family the obliteration of an *olam katan*, a *world-in-miniature.* Human words have not yet been devised with sufficient eloquence to console the grief-stricken family. Instead, there is a word of comfort from a higher source: the Sages, commenting on the scriptural word ‏"ויבא"‏, ''and he proceeded,'' ask: ''Whence did Abraham come?'' And they answered: ''From Mount Moriah''—that is, the exalted heights of Divine teaching and training! Abraham, in eulogizing his beloved wife, extolled Sarah's role as mother, which she had practiced with devotion and dignity. Isaac, who offered himself, his very life, for God, was the product of her maternal efforts. This was, indeed, the highest tribute of a grieving patriarch for his precious wife, his ''world-in-miniature'' that was taken from him.

Your wife and mother, ___________ ___________, was also a matriarch. She was blessed with the qualities of a Sarah who shared her faith, her wisdom and, above all, herself with her children. The beauty of her personality is reflected in the character of her children, and in the love of a husband devoted to her in her lifetime, who, like Abraham, is deeply wounded by the loss of his *olam katan*, his own ''world-in-minature.''

‏תהא נשמתה צרורה בצרור החיים‏

May her soul be bound up in the bond of eternal life, and may the bereaved family find comfort, not in well-turned phrases of praise, but in the beautiful memories of a precious and saintly life, an *olam katan*, a little world among the myriad ministering angels beyond the reach of mortal man.

‏שלום לעפרה‏

"The Root and the Fruit"

(For a parent whose children are praiseworthy)

אילן שנעקר ונשתיר בו שורש פטור (מערלה). וכמה יהא השורש? רבן שמעון בן גמליאל אומר משום רבי אליעזר בן יהודה איש ברתותא כמחט של מיתן (ערלה, פ״א, ד׳).

Jewish law designates the fruit of a young tree during the first three years as *orlah*, which may not be eaten. The same law applies to an uprooted tree that was replanted, because it loses its original identity. However, the tree is not considered uprooted and severed from its source if it remains attached, albeit by a tiny root no larger than a needle. In this instance, the *Mishnah* declares that a miniscule root preserves the original identity of the tree and exempts it from the restrictions of *orlah*.

We are assembled to mourn the loss of a beautiful tree whose sweet fruit nourished a generation of wonderful children. It is a tree pulled and torn by the ultimate tempest of death, but not entirely uprooted because not one but six roots firmly attach it to the source of life. You, his six precious children, sons and daughters in Israel, are the guarantors that your dear father will continue to live in your hearts and through your deeds and give spiritual sustenance to generations yet unborn. For you, Father lives on, and he will continue to live in your hopes, in your homes and in your works. Your way of life is a credit to your father, and your deeds proclaim for him the Jewish doctrine of life everlasting.

Your father's good work on earth was interrupted, not terminated, for you his devoted children, like the small roots in the *Mishnah*, bridge the yawning chasm between what was and what will be, eradicating death by affirming love and life. Your father's charitable work, kind words and pleasant disposition will find

renewal in your charitable work, kind words and pleasant disposition, and through your devotion will continue to bring forth
fruits of benevolence and love. Our Sages observed, ‏מה זרעו בחיים‎„
‏אף הוא בחיים‎" ''As his children live, he, too, lives on.''

May his memory ever be a blessing to the family and to those
he has touched with his warm heart and open hand. May his soul
rest in peace. Amen.

‏שלום לעפרו‎

"An Arsenal of Love"

(For a religious person with many virtues)

King David, in mourning the death of King Saul and his son Jonathan concluded his eulogy with the following words: איך נפלו גבורים ויאבדו כלי מלחמה "How are the mighty fallen and lost the instruments of war" (II Samuel 1:27). King David expressed in these words the profound loss of the first King of Israel.

Ordinarily, when a commander falls in battle, his weapons remain in the arsenal. If, however, a commander loses his life on the battlefield and the enemy succeeds also in capturing the ammunition, the loss is compounded.

We are assembled here to eulogize a fallen hero, a man whose faith was genuine, whose devotion to Torah was matchless, whose leadership was fruitful, whose interest in Jewish affairs was manifold. Fortunately, however, his ammunition has not been lost, for he leaves children who will continue to carry on in the spirit of their commander, their father.

Mr. ___________ ___________ bequeathed a great arsenal of lovingkindness, compassion, understanding and loyalty to Torah to our people and to our tradition. May his family find consolation in the knowledge that the ammunition of their father will remain for his loved ones to use in the battle for worthy causes and noble ideals.

שלום לעפרו

"The Divine Garden"

(For a child or youth; a gardner; a nature lover)

''My דודי ירד לגנו לערוגת הבשם לרעות בגנים וללקוט שושנים (שיר השירים, ו:ב) beloved is gone down to his garden, to the beds of spices, to feed in the gardens, and to gather lilies'' (Song of Songs 6:2).

When the gardener needs fruits he plucks those matured by age and ripened by time on branch and vine. However, when he seeks flowers, age and time play no role; quality of the fragrance alone determines the choice.

God, who created life lovingly and decreed that love is the essence of life, is known in Cantillations as דודי, ''my Beloved.'' He is the Gardener of the universe. Most often he lovingly plucks ripe old fruits, hoary-headed geezers, tired elderly people sated with life and yearning for rest.

Then there are those terrifying times, enigmatic and puzzling, when meaning and reason seem suspended and a mysterious cloud enshrouds our lives. That is when the Divine Gardener gathers flowers from His garden. The blooms are not chosen for their ripeness and age, but for their sweet fragrance. At that time, for reasons unintelligible to mere mortals, the Divine Gardener tenderly picks the redolent, the ambrosial, the most fragrant young flowers from His earthly garden to transplant them unspoiled in His Heavenly Garden of Eden in the company of saints and sages and the Heavenly Hosts.

With resignation and faith we bow to the divine decree. With resignation because God the Creator is the ultimate Judge. But also with faith, for he is דודי, ''my Beloved,'' teacher of kindness and author of love, whose lovingkindness does not cease even with bereavement and grief.

The sweet savor, the wonderful fragrance, the precious

memories remain for those who loved and pampered this flower. Let the heartbroken parents and family seek consolation in the knowledge that God chooses the best, the sweetest, the most fragrant for His Heavenly Garden.

In the words of Job: "The Lord gave, and the Lord hath taken away: may the name of the Lord be blessed" (Job 1:21).

שלום לעפרו

"Rooted and Fruitful"

(For a person with deep roots in the Jewish tradition who
reared children loyal to their roots and their heritage)

"למה הוא דומה? לאילן שענפיו מועטין ושרשיו מרובין, שאפילו כל הרוחות שבעולם
באות ונושבות בו, אין מזיזין אותו ממקומו, שנאמר: „והיה כעץ שתול על מים ועל יובל
ישלח שרשיו ולא יראה כי יבא חם, והיה עליהו רענן ובשנת בצרת לא ידאג ולא ימיש
מעשות פרי'" (ירמי', י"ז, ח')

A deep-rooted tree is often admired for its ability to withstand
wind and storm. At times, a tree may be extolled for its nourishing
and delicious fruit.

Such praise and admiration may be extended to human beings
as well. One person deserves our respect for his spiritually rooted
and culturally rich heritage deeply grounded in Torah study and
traditional values; another equally deserving individual is noted
for having inspired his children to follow the adaptive and
redemptive path of *mitzvot* and ethical/moral values. Each one of
them merits high grades and sincere appreciation for a valuable
contribution to תיקון העולם and דרכי שלום, social improvement and
human perfection.

However, the blessed but rare phenomenon of a person who
successfully combines and synthesizes both commendable qualities evokes our highest gratitude and admiration. What finer
paradigm of penultimate human potential than a person deeply
rooted in the heritage of his faith, whose children, the sweet fruit
of a lifetime of diligent, caring, gentle guidance, remain consistently faithful to the genetic formula of the differentiated natural
plant species reflecting honorably on the trunk and the branches
and the roots—and the generations of faithful trees in the genetic
background of that tree. Such a tree deserves, with every justifica-

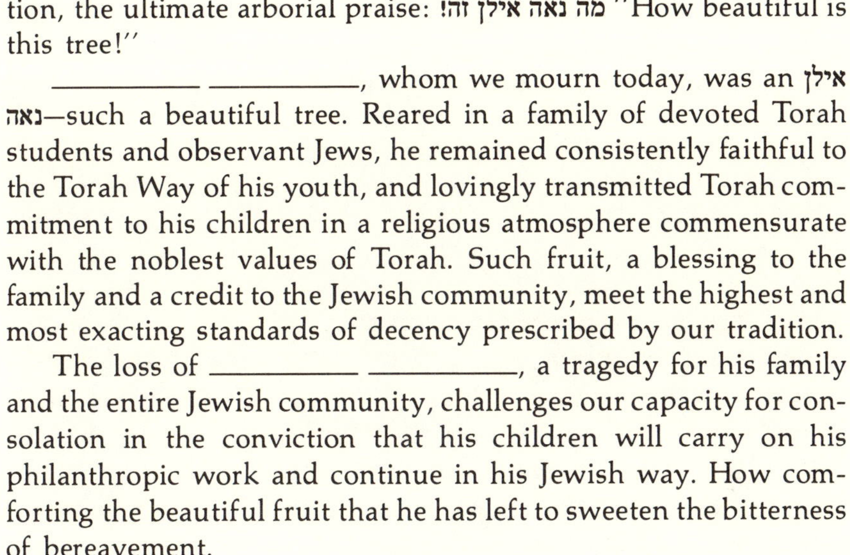

tion, the ultimate arborial praise: ‏מה נאה אילן זה!‏ ''How beautiful is this tree!''

__________ __________, whom we mourn today, was an ‏אילן נאה‏—such a beautiful tree. Reared in a family of devoted Torah students and observant Jews, he remained consistently faithful to the Torah Way of his youth, and lovingly transmitted Torah commitment to his children in a religious atmosphere commensurate with the noblest values of Torah. Such fruit, a blessing to the family and a credit to the Jewish community, meet the highest and most exacting standards of decency prescribed by our tradition.

The loss of __________ __________, a tragedy for his family and the entire Jewish community, challenges our capacity for consolation in the conviction that his children will carry on his philanthropic work and continue in his Jewish way. How comforting the beautiful fruit that he has left to sweeten the bitterness of bereavement.

‏שלום לעפרו‏

''Three Witnesses''

(For a consistently fine person with a reputable public image
and a sterling reputation as a husband, father and human
being)

„יהי מקורך ברוך.׳ מכאן אמרו אשרי אדם שאשתו מעידו, תורתו מעידו. פרנסתו
מעידו. ועליו הכתוב אומר: ,יהי מקורך ברוך׳״ (משלי, ה׳ י״ח). [ילקוט שמעוני משלי,
ה׳,י״ח] '''Let thy fountain be blessed.''' From this (the Sages) said:
happy is the man whose wife testifies for him, whose Torah testifies for him, whose business testifies for him. Concerning him,
scripture says: 'Let thy fountain be blessed''' (*Yalkut Shimoni*,
Mishlei 5).

Society's popular evaluation of an individual is derived from a
visual assessment of that person. We tend to rely on subjective
observation when calculating character and personality. As a
consequence of this superficial estimation of human worth, many
ostensibly fine and ''upright'' members of the community are, in
fact, delinquent in their obligations to spouse and children. Renowned public servants are not necessarily paragons of virtue in
their private lives; scholarship and piety do not guarantee in the
spheres of personal concern. Indeed, as far as they are concerned,
charity does *not* begin at home!

Our Sages, however, offered lustrous counsel in their fabulous
formula for the evaluation of an unfamiliar individual.

The first and most credible witness is a person's wife.
Equipped with intimate data, special insights and feminine sen-
sitivities, she knows the truth about her husband, and her testimony reflects the facts of his life. Her testimony, e.g., that he is
the best husband in the world, is admissible as a valid private
analogue to a favorable public image.

Similarly, Torah scholarship, if it is to be respected, must be reflected in character and behavior, just as religious commitment must find expression in honest business practices, ethical values and moral standards.

__________ __________ synthesized the three criteria in the rabbinic test for true stature in the community. His dear wife __________ loved and admired him. Their married life was a privilege of affection and devotion. His benevolence and philanthropy were deeply rooted in and derived from a genuine respect for Torah scholarship and authentic Jewish erudition. Finally, his peerless reputation as an honest and reliable businessman was a veritable *Kiddush Hashem*, a sanctification of God's Name, and a model in the industry.

The tribute of the three witnesses to __________ __________ is the most beautiful panegyric, the most eloquent eulogy, a credible encomium without parallel.

תהא נשמתו צרורה בצרור החיים.

May the soul of __________ __________ be bound up in the bond of eternal life, and may the Supreme judge grant consolation to his bereaved and heartbroken family.

שלום לעפרו

"Not Leaving Empty-Handed"

(For a very charitable person; also fitting during the week of פרשת
שמות)

„ונתתי את חן העם הזה בעיני מצרים, והיה כי תלכון לא תלכו ריקם" (שמות, ג,
כא). "And I will give this people favor in the sight of the
Egyptians. And it shall come to pass that when ye go, ye shall
not go empty (handed)" (Exodus 3:21).

The Lord promised Moses that when they left the Land of
Bondage the Israelites would not go away empty-handed; they
would leave wealthy, laden with many precious things.

Here is a poignant message for all times. In a sense, this
world is a Land of Bondage for all men, and we, the bondsmen, are
enslaved to multiplex needs and sundry desires, temptations and
lusts, materialistic blandishments and egotistical vanities,
ephemeral illusions and evanescent ambitions. Money and honor,
in large measure, determine the quality and direction of life.

However, when the time comes for a person to depart this
world, the universal Land of Bondage, to be liberated from the
tyranny of things and be free (which is, after all, the meaning of
נפטר) of life's shackles that kept him bound to crass, mundane
concerns, it is important that he not go away on his journey into
eternity empty-handed.

——————— ———————, to whom we pay our last respects
today, will be remembered by us all for his open hand and kind
heart. He does not depart this world empty-handed. His hands,
always extended in friendship, graciously distributed uncounted
sums of charity for *yeshivot*, all communal institutions and every
needy person who asked for help, and they are laden with the
precious treasures that are God's cash receipts and scrips for a
lifetime of goodness and love.

צדק לפניו יהלך
His charitable deeds shall precede him in Heaven.

שלום לעפרו

"The Musical Key of Inner Conflict"

(For a man who resisted life's temptations and remained steadfast in his loyalty to his faith and its traditions; for a musician; for a man named Joseph)

Three words in the Book of Bereishit are graced with the rare and exotic cantillation of שלשלת (*shalshelet*). They are:

1. ויתמהמה, "and, while he lingered" (Genesis 19:16);
2. ויאמר, "and he said" (Ibid., 24:12); and
3. וימאן, "But he refused" (Ibid., 39:8).

The *shalshelet* is not a *spianato* or smooth sound, but a *stridente*, zigzag musical formula denoting the emotional turbulence in the life of the person uttering the *shalshelet*-connected word.

The first person with a *shalshelet* modifier was Lot, who acquired this musical distinction when he departed from his uncle Abraham. Lot had surveyed the fertile plain in the vicinity of Sodom and Gomorrah and looked forward to great wealth and a life of comfort. Suddenly, he is ordered to give up his dream of luxurious abundance and a life of ease and flee for his life because of an approaching disaster. Lot is not emotionally prepared to surrender his ambitious aspiration for mundane success. Doubts about the credibility of the angelic message begin to gnaw at his credulity. In this state of inner turmoil, Lot is paralyzed. ויתמהמה, he waits. And the *shalshelet* on that word underscores the ectopic conflict raging in his soul.

The second *shalshelet*-connected individual is Eliezer. Abraham had charged his faithful steward with the noble task of selecting a wife for Isaac. As the story unfolds, Eliezer stands near the well, depressed and dejected, skeptical about the outcome of his mission. Wavering in confidence, he decides to gamble on several arbitrary signs of etiquette and courtesy as reliable indicators of the girl's acceptability into the Hebrew household. Eliezer inwardly questions the validity of his "test" and the *shalshelet* over „ויאמר", betrays the internal turbulence troubling his benevolent heart.

The third *shalshelet* intrudes during a critical episode in the life of Joseph. Reared in the strictly traditional home in which he enjoyed his father's love and favor, he tastes the bitter dregs of fraternal jealousy, enmity and, finally, violence. Sold into servitude, he is forcibly taken by his Ishmaelite captors to Egypt where he is acquired as a slave by a prominent Egyptian, the chamberlain in Pharaoh's court. A foreigner in a strange land and a slave, though respected, he barely begins to adjust to his new status and exotic environment when the master's wife resolves to seduce him. The temptation is great, but Joseph is sustained in his moral struggle by the vision of his father, דמות דקיונו של אביו, and he flees from his master's luxurious home and the lure of beguiling, covinous and seductive immorality. Joseph's selfless, heroic act earned him the title צדיק, saint, and וימאן, the terse token of his stubborn refusal to betray his master and his own moral code, is adorned with a *shalshelet*, reflecting the intense struggle and tempestuous conflict that occurred in Joseph's youthful heart.

The life of __________ __________, whom we mourn today, was crowned with more than one *shalshelet*. Reared in a traditional Jewish home, he remained constantly and consistently loyal to Torah principles and precepts that he incorporated into his own home. The vision of his sainted father and mother guided him throughout his life as he heroically and steadfastly struggled against the myriad temptations to compromise religious values. He never yielded to seductive promises of material gain at the price of Shabbat, *kashruth* and business ethics. The fierce inner conflict of an honest American businessman earned him many a *shalshelet*, and, like Joseph of old, he genuinely deserves the title, צדיק.

May the memory of _________ _________ be a living

memorial to his wife and children, to his entire family and to all of us who were privileged to know and admire him.

זכר צדיק לברכה
The memory of the righteous is a blessing.

"The Blessing of the Priest"

לז״נ אמו״ר ר׳ יוסף ב״ר יחיאל הכהן ז״ל
In memory of my beloved father

by Hershel Cohen

(For a rabbi, a *kohen* or a communal leader)

תורת אמת היתה בפיהו ועולה לא נמצא בשפתיו בשלום ובמישור הלך אתי
ורבים השיב מעון (מלאכי ב,ו). "The law of truth was in his mouth,
and iniquity was not found in his lips; he walked with me in
peace and equity, and did turn many from iniquity" (Malachi
2,6).

The prophet Malachi offers an ethical description of the first
kohen, Aaron, his son Eliezer and his grandson Pinchas.

"The law of truth was in his mouth" underscores the virtue
of global honesty. The double standard of אחד בפה ואחד בלב is not
acceptable to the prophet's standard of righteousness. Heart and
mouth must conform to the same coordinate.

"He walked with me in peace and equity." His every deed
was לשם שמים, not for self-glorification or personal gain, but for a
noble purpose, and always to sow peace and harmony wherever
he went.

"And did turn away from iniquity." A man of love and compassion, he lovingly and compassionately led many straying souls
back to God.

This endearing and enduring portrait of the first priestly
family in Israel also describes another *kohen*, the deceased to
whom we are bidding farewell today. ___________ ___________ was
a man of truth. He adhered to the highest principles of honesty,
and his heart was pure. He loved peace and equity and taught
these virtues by example. He created a moral climate in the community in which harmony and love flourished. With love, kind

words and compassionate understanding, he brought scores of dejected and rejected men and women back to *yiddishkeit* and the Torah Way of Life. His sincerity, integrity and humility testified to his Godliness.

__________ __________ wore the three crowns mentioned in Pirke Avoth with dignity. The crowns of Torah, *Kehuna* and *Shem Tov* fit him naturally. A genuine Torah scholar, humble and self-effacing, he wore his priestly crown with silent elegance and his name became a blessing in every Jewish home. During a lifetime of selfless and devoted service to the community, __________ __________ won the hearts of all who knew him, and they showered him with genuine love and admiration. His heavy burden of obligations and a busy schedule devoted to communal work did not isolate him from his people. On the contrary, he became even busier, sharing with hundreds of families their joys and their sorrows. His door was always open to visitors in need of advice, a word of comfort or a sympathetic ear.

Above all was his profound love of Torah. Influenced by the Torah world from which he drew his nurture, he sensed a personal mission to fulfill the ideal of ללמוד וללמד to study Torah and to share it with others. He dedicated every opportunity to Torah study and consecrated the most esoteric moments to the teaching of Torah to others. A gifted public speaker of rare eloquence and cogency, his finest sermons were preached not with the lips, but with his heart—and life. For he was the priest who did more than bless his people; *he* was their blessing.

שלום לעפרו

"Perfection from Head to Toe"

(For a very observant person who lived a life devoted to piety and good deeds; for a man named Jacob; for the *sidrah Vayeḥi*)

"He ויאסוף רגליו אל המטה ויגוע ויאסף אל עמיו (בראשית, מ"ט, ל"ג) gathered up his feet into the bed, and expired and was gathered unto his people" (Genesis 49:33).

A person may be fanatical about his grooming and extremely cautious about his wardrobe. His garments are spotless—yet his shoes pick up the dust and dirt of the floor, unless he walks on immaculate floors or scrupulously cleaned carpets. Similarly, no matter how observant and careful a person is about his spiritual life, he will, albeit innocently and unintentionally, pick up some environmental contamination.

The religious experience is no different. An impeccable spiritual life is no unconditional guarantee of perfection. Even the most observant occasionally trespass, innocently. שגיאות מי יבין מנסתרות נקני (תהילים, י"ט, י"ג) "Who can guard against errors? From secret faults do Thou cleanse me" (Psalms 19,13)

It is difficult, if not impossible, to engage in business and the professions—or simply to be a part of the real world—without some dust particles adhering to one's feet.

Jacob was an exception. When, on his death bed, „ויאסוף רגליו אל המטה" "he gathered up his feet into the bed," he demonstrated to his assembled children that all his life he walked in God's path and faithfully followed His commands, that his feet were unsoiled and unsullied by sin and greed.

——————— ——————— was another rare exception among men, a genuinely religious person whose feet never trod the ways of sin. Like Jacob, his spiritual life drew a fine and generous balance between duties toward God and obligations to man. If Jacob the Patriarch earned an אבל גדול, great mourning,

__________ __________ too deserves to be mourned exceedingly, for the loss of a person of his religious-spiritual-ethical configuration—one who is spiritually clean from head to *feet*—is irreplaceable.

שלום לעפרו

"Mourning in the Market Place"

(For a respected merchant, philanthropist or public spirited person)

''Because כי הולך האדם אל בית עולמו וסבבו בשוק הסופדים (קהלת י"ב, ה') man goeth to his long home, and the mourners go about the streets (market place).''

The death of a loved one is a very personal loss and the bereavement experienced by wife, children, relatives and close friends underscores man's acute vulnerability to loneliness and isolation. The eulogy in the funeral chapel appropriately focuses on the life of the deceased. The market place, far from the chapel, is oblivious to the tragedy, and those who are at a distance from the funeral service go about their daily tasks unaware of the grief that has overwhelmed a local family.

On the other hand, when people in the market place, far from the funeral chapel, bewail the loss, it is a sign that they mourn for a dear friend, a person who cared and provided for them.

___________ ___________, whom we eulogize today, is a man who will be missed not only by his bereaved wife, children, relatives and friends, but by the many needy families upon whom he lavished time, compassion and financial assistance. Yes, he is mourned in the market place, far from here, where he was loved for his warmhearted kindness, honored for his mercantile skill and respected for his uncompromising standards of business ethics.

The mourning in the market place is his most eloquent eulogy.

שלום לעפרו

"Too Tragic For Words"

(For a child whose parents are bereaved beyond consolation)

The *Tikunei Zohar* relates that when the Second Temple was destroyed, both Zion and Jerusalem sought the privilege of delivering the eulogy and bewailing the disaster that had befallen the Jewish people.

Jerusalem maintained that she could be more objective because Zion was too close to the Temple Mount. Zion, it was claimed, could not muster the vocabulary needed to eulogize the Sanctuary or the proper words for dirges adequate to bemoan the debacle.

Zion, however, argued that verbal expression of grief over the חורבן was not necessary. An אנחה—a sigh or a groan—would convey more grieving than mere words.

We who are assembled here to share the grief and anguish of a mother and father struck by a personal חורבן, the loss of a precious son (daughter), find ourselves in the position of Zion. For years, we were so close to the family, sharing in their joys, their hopes and their dreams. Like Zion, we are too close to the __________ family, too intimately connected, to express our sorrow in formal phrases and well-intentioned words. Our hearts, too, are broken, our souls seared and sickened by the tragedy. Like Zion, the only eulogy we can summon up is a sigh and a groan from the depth of our heart and soul. The bereaved parents, family and good friends will, no doubt, discern an echo of their own anguish in the agonized lament of our broken hearts. Soon, they will know that they do not grieve alone.

May the __________ family find some measure of consolation in the fact that the entire community mourns with them. And even as the destruction of the Temple did not put an end to our people, so will the memory of ___________ ___________ endure against all the storms of time. Ultimately, the eulogies of both Zion and Jerusalem will be fulfilled.

May God comfort you together with all the mourners of *Zion* and *Jerusalem.*

שלום לעפרו

"Unforgettable—Like an Olive Tree"

(For a saintly person distinguished by a good name, charitable deeds and communal leadership)

כל זית שיש לו שם בשדה אפילו כזית הנטופה בשעתו ושכחו אינו שכחה. בד"א בשמו, ובמעשיו ובמקומו (פאה, פרק ז', א') "An olive tree that has a distinguishing name in the field, like the olive tree of Netufa in its season, and that has been left forgotten, is not deemed 'forgotten'. When does this stipulation apply? [Only to a tree that is distinguished] by its name, or its produce, or its situation [or position]." (Pe'ah, ch 7, Mishnah 1).

The special qualities that render an olive tree "unforgettable" and immune to the laws of שכחה were the beautiful character traits that distinguished _________ _________ as a saintly and unforgettable person.

בד"א? בשמו. "When does this apply? Only to a tree that is distinguished by its name." _________ _________ was distinguished by a name respected for honesty and associated with the finest moral, ethical and social traits, a name that brings pleasant connotations and recollections to family, friends, neighbors and business associates.

ובמעשיו. "or its produce." _________ _________'s מעשים or good deeds brought much love and healing to countless broken hearts and shattered spirits. His dedicated voluntary and philanthropic work in behalf of almost every worthy charitable institution in this state reflected nobly on his belief that "faith" and "love" are best realized, not in theory, but in practice. _________ _________ will be long remembered by those whose mended lives bear eloquent testimony to the validity of his "produce" philosophy or theology.

ובמקומו. "or its place (or position)." _________ _________ occupied a special place in the Jewish community. Sensitive to the needs of people and the limited resources of the social agencies to meet these needs, he worked assiduously for the most equitable and democratic formulas by which communal responsibility could be met in the most gracious way. __________ __________ was always concerned for the integrity of the community and its philanthropic agencies. He did, indeed, occupy a very distinguished place in the community, a place that must remain vacant not because of a dearth of worthy contenders, but because __________ __________ was so very singular and special.

We know that no consoling words can assuage the pain of the bereaved family. However, I can assure you that שכחה, forgetfulness, does not apply to the memory of __________ __________. Like the olive tree, __________ __________ will always be lovingly remembered by his family, his congregation and the entire community. We all share your grief and anguish, and want you to know that __________ __________ cannot be forgotten because his name, a "good name [that] is better than good oil," will be enshrined forever in our synagogue, the communal institutions he led and supported, and—in our hearts.

May the God of mercy comfort you in full measure among those who mourn for Zion and Jerusalem.

שלום לעפרו

"A Celebration of Life"

ז״נ אבי מורי ר׳ אברהם אלחנן ב״ר דוב הלוי ת׳נ׳צ׳ב׳ה׳
Dedicated to the memory of my beloved father
Abraham Solomon

by Victor M. Solomon

(For a father who leaves worthy children;
for a man named Abraham).

ואמר רב חנן בר רבא אמר רב: אותו היום שנפטר אברהם אבינו מן העולם עמדו
כל גדולי אומות העולם בשורה ואמרו: ,אוי לו לעולם שאבד מנהיגו ואוי לה
לספינה שאבד קברינטא׳" (בבא בתרא, צא ע״א-ע״ב)

The Talmud relates: "Rav Hanan bar Rava further said in the
name of Rav: On the day when Abraham our father passed away
from the world all the great ones of the nations of the world, stood
in line [it was the custom for those who came to offer comfort to
mourners to stand in line—Ed.) and said: Woe is to the world that
has lost its leader and woe is to the ship that has lost its pilot."
(Baba Bathra, 91a,b).

The Gerer Rebbe offered a penetrating comment on this Talmudic passage. The heathen world, he said, was prepared to close
the "Book of Abraham" and to consider his life's work, his
aspirations and his mission at an end. This view determined the
choice of metaphor—"אוי לה לספינה שאבד קברינטא„ "Woe is to the
ship that has lost its pilot"—selected by the heathen political
leadership. They simply reported with candor what was known
by all dispassionate phenomenologic observers. When a naval
pilot or captain dies and is buried at sea, his body is swallowed up
by the waves and he disappears into oblivion in an unmarked
grave in the depths of the sea, leaving no trace of remembrance.
Death, they believed, ultimately triumphs over life, erasing the
past, obliterating hopes, and devouring dreams and, finally, the
meaning of life.

However, the proponents of heathen philosophy did not reckon with the Jewish metaphysical view of life and death. In the Jewish configuration, Abraham did not disappear into an unmarked grave like a ship's pilot because Isaac was his memorial. Abraham's faith and dreams became a way of life for generations of Jews, loyal sons and daughters of Abraham our father, who measured life from ancestral antiquity to glorious destiny. Indeed, the Jew who identifies with the Jewish faith affirms and confirms Abraham's immortality.

Thus, two generations after Abraham, the same Jewish metaphysical view of life prompted the observation in the Talmud that Jacob, too, did not die: „מה זרעו בחיים אף הוא בחיים"

We have come here today, not so much to mourn the death of ______________ ______________ as to celebrate the life of a devoted father whose wonderful children, whom he cherished with so much love and delight, are his living memorial. Like Isaac, they affirm that his memory will live on in the hearts and in the Jewish lives of upcoming generations. Who can ask for anything more!

תהא נשמתו צרורה בצרור החיים

May his soul be bound up in the bond of eternal life.

"The Vital Signs of Life"

(For a charitable, popular person
who was active in the community)

''His „פניו כלפי העם סימן יפה לו; כלפי הכותל סימן רע לו." (כתובות ק"ג:)
face towards the public it is a good omen, towards the wall it
is a bad omen'' (Kethuboth, 103b).

Jewish law requires one who finds a lost object to publicize it, provided it has סימנים, identifiable signs. The absence of such signs exempts the finder from this obligation.

The huge assembly gathered in this chapel today bears eloquent testimony to the sorrow of the community over the loss of a precious constituent. Since it is mandatory, according to Jewish law, to publicize the סימנים of a lost object, it behooves us, in this instance too, to reveal the signs of a precious person whose loss you have come to mourn.

Our Sages provided a variety of signs by which one could be identified as a person worthy of being created in the image of God. This ''personality key'' includes, among other signs, the direction he faced when he died. If his face was turned toward the people, it is a good sign for him. If, however, his face is turned toward the wall, then it is a bad sign for him.

Our Sages were conveying a message about the vital signs of life that are the symbolic litmus test of a person's spiritual worth. They proposed two intimately related principles. First, an individual either faces the people or the wall, i.e., he either is concerned for others and cares for the community or turns his back on the world, looking only after his own selfish concerns. Second, there is both a positive and a negative consistency in human nature: the way a person dies reflects the way he lived.

_______________ _____________ was a person who faced the people all his life. Active in every community endeavor, true to the highest ideals of social responsibility and devoted to the needs of the "weaker vessels," the deprived and the disenfranchised, _________ _________ left the world as he had lived in it, kind, caring and loving. Few can equal his generosity. He lived with an open hand and died with a clearly defined *sign* of nobility.

שלום לעפרו

"The End of Days . . . But Life Everlasting"

(For a scholar, author, writer, composer, musician, artist, creative
person)

„הן קרבו ימיך למות, (דברים ל"א:י"ד) ימים מתים אבל צדיקים אינם מתים.
ויקרבו ימי ישראל למות, (בראשית מ"ז:כ"ט). ,ויקרבו ימי דוד למות," (מלכים
א', ב:א) [בראשית רבה] '' 'Behold, thy days approach that thou
must die' (Deuteronomy 31:14). 'Days' die but the righteous
do not die. 'And the time (*days*) drew near that Israel must
die.' (Genesis 47:29) 'Now the *days* of David drew nigh that
he should die.''' (I Kings 2:1) [Genesis Rabba].

What is the true purpose of a eulogy? Is it to help us deal
with the stark tragedy of bereavement (derived from a Frisian
term meaning robbery), that we have sustained a terrible loss, that
a loved one was "stolen" from us and we shall be deprived of his
company forever? If this be the only reason for the ritual, then it
would be a decidedly personal, if not an intrinsically selfish matter. We must, therefore, reject shallow, facile definitions in favor
of a deeper, more challenging explanation out of respect for the
enormity of the tragedy that has befallen the family and the
Jewish community.

We are assembled here today to mourn the muting of the
muse, the diminution of creativity, the extinction of the rhap-
sodic. Were ___________ ___________ still among us, he would
share with us, generously, from his inexhaustible store of wisdom
and creative genius. We are mourning our impoverishment, the
loss of his valuable counsel and inspiration, the prolific products
of a towering intellect.

There is, however, a drop of solace in the bitter cup of tears.
It is the ancient biblical assurance that individuals of ___________
___________'s *esprit* do not die. Only their *days* are cancelled.
Their wisdom and creative genius remain enshrined in libraries—

and in the hearts of the disciples of the wise. *Tzadikim*, too, never die. Their voices ring forth in the company of the righteous and in the corridors of time, encouraging the meek, enriching the poor and challenging the astute.

To all of us who loved and admired ___________ ___________, and to his grieving family, may these reflections bring a measure of consolation.

שלום לעפרו

"Only God Can Make a Tree ... But Man Must Care For It"

(For an immigrant who remained steadfast in his Jewish commitments and loyal to the religious ideals of his parents)

„והיה כעץ שתול על פלגי מים אשר פריו יתן בעתו ועלהו לא יבול וכל אשר
יעשה יצליח.״ (תהילים א:ג)

"And he shall be like a tree planted by streams of water,
That bringeth forth its fruit in its season,
And whose leaf doth not wither;
And in whatsoever he doeth he shall prosper." (Psalms 1:3)

There are two Hebrew terms for planting. One refers to the planting of seeds and is called *Netiah.* The other relates to transplanting a tree or sapling from elsewhere in new soil and is called *Shetilah.*

The psalmist compares the *tzadik* to an *eitz shatul,* a transplanted tree, a rhetorical choice fraught with special meaning for us today.

The older generation of American Jews were mainly transplanted trees, uprooted from their native lands, mostly in Eastern and Central Europe, and transplanted, if not gently, in the rich, nourishing soil of our blessed America. They had left those lands in which their forebears had lived for centuries and developed a magnificent religious civilization-in-exile. They had also left behind or lost at sea much of their spiritual heritage. What they did manage to preserve was sequentially ravaged by acculturation and assimilation. These newcomers failed to transmit a sense of excitement about, pride in and unalloyed devotion to the faith of their parents. Their roots did not penetrate deeply enough to sustain a new generation from old sources of spiritual sustenance that had nourished our people throughout the millennia. Their children, planted in strange fields, untouched by the "blessed rains'' (גשמי ברכה) and the ''heavenly dew'' (טל השמים) grew wild and uncultivated, distant, for the most part, from the refreshing wellsprings of Torah and *mitzvot.*

In this sad and somber moment, it is a delight to declare before this solemn assembly that ___________ ___________ was a veritable *eitz shatul* in this land, in the finest denotation and connotation of that term. Availing himself fully of the wonderful opportunities offered by this ''Golden Land,'' ___________ ___________ never diminished his Jewish identity or compromised his religious commitments. To the end, ___________ ___________ synthesized his pride in his American citizenship with a fierce loyalty to his Jewish heritage. A successful and committed businessman, ___________ ___________ always found time for Torah, study, synagogue and prayer.

אשרי האיש—Happy is the man who walks in the way of the righteous. Concerning him we can say צדיק באמונתו יחיה, the ''righteous *lives* by his faith,'' and add the blessing: בורא פרי העץ confident that the quality of the tree is reflected in the children who will also walk in the path of a worthy father.

שלום לעפרו

"*Perpetual Care*"

(For a person who endowed a philanthropic institution or left a trust fund for a synagogue or a bequest for the perpetuation of Torah scholarship)

„וְלֹא יֵרָאוּ פָנַי רֵיקָם, (שמות לד:כ) אפילו לאחר מיתה" (ירושלמי, חגיגה, פ״א הל׳ א') "'And none shall appear before Me empty' (Exodus 34:20) even after death" (Jerusalem Talmud, Hagigah, Ch I, Halakhah 1).

Our Sages admired the charitable, generous philanthropist and esteemed the person who shared his material blessings with those less fortunate during his lifetime. They went a step further, transcending conventional modes of philanthropy, praising the individual who shares his wealth after he is called to his heavenly rest.

The Jerusalem Talmud, commenting on the verse in Exodus 34:20, "And none shall appear before Me empty," postulated that the ideal charity is that which continues to do good beyond one's mortal span of years. When a person endows a philanthropic institution, or establishes a trust fund for a synagogue, or leaves a bequest for the perpetuation of Jewish scholarship, he affirms his faith in the truly Jewish view of philanthropy.

——————— ——————— genuinely fulfilled this Torah ideal. He shared his fortune with others during a lifetime devoted to the noblest Jewish paradigm of benevolence—and left a trust fund to continue his charitable work in behalf of *yeshivot* and other worthy institutions beyond his allotted time on earth.

——————— ——————— will surely come into the presence of God, not empty-handed, but full of צדק חסד. For his concern for Torah and people was not limited by the usual constraints of time and life; he truly believed in "perpetual caring."

שלום לעפרו

"A Global Loss"

(For a kind and compassionate person)

„הצדיק אָבָד ואין איש שם על לב ואנשי חסד נאספים באין מבין כי מפני הרעה
נאסף הצדיק." (ישעי' נז:א) "The righteous perisheth, and no man
layeth it to heart; and merciful (i.e., kind) men are taken
away, none considering that the righteous is taken away from
that which is evil" (Isaiah 57:1).

The prophet Isaiah arraigns an apathetic public that impassively condones the death of the righteous, without dissent or
protest. This cynical insouciance and moral detachment could be
forgiven in the context of the *tzadik*'s personality. Few ever
penetrate the aura of his inverted discipline and self-sacrifice. The
tzadik lived in the four cubits of Torah and *mitzvot*, oblivious to
world issues and universal problems. He was not involved in
communal affairs and maintained a respectful distance from the
contaminating influences ordinary men and women must confront every day. His presence was not felt when he lived, and he
was not missed after he died.

What torments the prophet is the agonizing fact that *Anshei
Ḥesed* passed on and the tragedy was lost on the people of his
generation. Kind and compassionate souls, the core of communal
life, were taken from their midst and the spiritual vacuum was
unnoticed—מפני הרעה—because of the moral decay and corruption
of a society that does not weep when kind and compassionate
Anshei Ḥesed pass away!

As we pay our last respects to ___________ ___________ we,
unlike Isaiah's contemporaries, *do* feel the loss of a חסיד, a fine and
gentle human being. We keenly perceive a baneful communal
tragedy as well as a painful bereavement for the family. It will
come as no surprise to the family, and as a source of consolation,
that the entire Jewish community shares their grief and
anguish—.צרת רבים חצי נחמה

______________ ______________ left a beautiful legacy of decency and love. And the Jewish community, upon whom he lavished his kindness, will always remember him kindly and will cherish his name forever.

תהא נשמתו צרורה בצרור החיים

"The Ledger and the Key"

(For a poor but decent person, or one who was childless and lived a virtuous life)

„וכשמת שמואל הקטן תלו מפתחו ופנקסו בארונו מפני שלא היה לו בן. והיה
רבן גמליאל ור' אלעזר (בן עזריה) מספידין עליו ואומרים 'על זה נאה לבכות, על
זה נאה להתאבל, מלכים מתים ומניחין כתריהם לבניהם, עשירים מתים ומניחים
עושר לבניהם. שמואל הקטן נטל כל החמודות שבעולם והלך לו.' " (מס' שמחות
פרק ח'.) "When Shmuel Hakatan died, they hung his key and
his ledger on his coffin because he had no son. And Rabban
Gamliel and R. Elazar (ben Azaria) eulogized him saying 'for
such a one it is fitting to weep, on such a one it is fitting to
mourn. Kings die and leave their crowns to their sons.
Wealthy people die and leave their wealth to their sons.
Shmuel Hakatan took all the desirable things in the world
and went his way.'" (Semahot, 8)

Every person goes through life with a *pinkas*, or ledger, to
keep an account of his deeds and a *mafteah*, or key, with which to
open doors. The righteous individual records in his notebook all
his praiseworthy accomplishments, his hours devoted to worship
and Torah study and his work in behalf of *yeshivot* and other
vital institutions in the community. With the key, the concerned
and caring Jew with a sense of history and destiny opens doors of
institutions that perpetuate Torah and serve the needs of the
elderly, the infirm, the orphaned and the poor. Sometimes, the
key is used to open the frozen hearts of those who live only for
themselves, to enable noble feelings to enter and warm their souls.
Such keepers of the ledger and the key use their instruments wise-
ly and to virtuous advantage.

Unfortunately, these spiritually advantaged individuals are
the exception. As a rule, people tend to trivialize their records and
to use their keys to open Pandora's boxes of gossip about another
person's faults and envy of a neighbor's financial success. Their

children could, very well, inherit impressive worldly possessions and great wealth, but such mundane estates and portfolios are but trivia in the world to come, a travesty in the context of genuine, eternal values. Can an inheritance of worldly, tangible ephemerals compensate for a legacy of embarrassing emptiness documented by a mockingly captious ledger and a cancelled key?

Shmuel Hakatan filled his ledger with lines that witnessed a life gloriously lived, and with his key he opened minds to wisdom and hearts to Torah and *mitzvot*. He, thus, earned the honor to be eulogized by spiritual giants like Rabban Gamliel and Rabbi Elazar (ben Azariah) who testified publicly to the propriety of mourning and weeping for a person of Shmuel Hakatan's caliber. He left no children, but his ledger and key symbolized a magnificent heritage of spiritual and moral treasures that he bequeathed to the collective posterity of mankind.

__________ ___________, whom we eulogize today, was such a person. He filled the pages of his ledger with endless entries of *maasim tovim*, good deeds, and he used his key to open his heart and meager resources to the cries of the needy and unlatched the hearts of others to the appeals of conscience. _________ _________ left no impressive bank books or keys to tempting vaults and safety deposit boxes. What he did leave for all of us is the key to the mystery of the *tzelem Elokim*, the *imago dei*, the divine image that distinguishes man from other creatures, and an inspiring narrative in his ledger of life, which is the most eloquent tribute to a wonderful human being. For __________ __________, as for Shmuel Hakatan, it is fitting, in the words of Rabban Gamliel and Rabbi Elazar (ben Azariah), to weep and preach eulogies.

May his *pinkas* and *mafteah*, his ledger, and his key, be a *melitz yosher* for his wife and family, and for all those who will miss him deeply.

שלום לעפרו

"Moist Like Moses"

(For one who lived a long vigorous life without illness or enfeeble-
ment; for a man named Moshe)

„ומשה בן מאה ועשרים שנה במתו לא כהתה עיניו ולא נס לֵחֹה" [רש"י מוסיף:
ולא נס לֵחֹה — לחלוחית שבו] (דברים לד:ז') [עיין סוטה י"ג:]. ''And
Moses was a hundred and twenty years old when he died; his
eye was not dim, nor his natural force abated'' [Rashi adds:
leicho denotes the freshness (lit. ''moisture'') within him]
(Deuteronomy 34:7) [Sotah, 13b].

The Torah in eulogizing Moses cites his physical characteristics, the excellent vision of his eyes and his fresh and hydrated
body. The Torah's choice of these two physical conditions for
special attention seems rather odd in view of the many virtues of
Moses that secured his unique place in history.

On closer examination, the choice is both justified and
appropriate for a vital didactic message. It piquantly postulates an
important epigrammatic formula: attachment to God and an
unconditional commitment to His precepts as a way of life keeps
one eternally young and vigorous—ואתם הדבקים בה' אלקיכם חיים כלכם
היום. (דברים ד:ד). ''You who cling unto the Lord your God are all
alive today.'' (Deuteronomy 4:4).

Moses, the *ish ha-elokim*, the Godly man, who devoted his
life to God and His commandments escaped the stress and deterioration that characterize old age. He retained the endowments of
youthful freshness, vigor and moisture characteristic of the
lechem hapanim, the twelve loaves of the sacred shewbread that
never became stale from the day they were placed by the priests
on the *shulchan hazahav*, the Golden Table in the Sanctuary, until
they were removed a week later.

סילוקו כסידורו

The Torah revealed in the person of Moses a singular type of
Jew, a ''fresh'' person, a ''moisted'' Jew, if you will, who is spared

the stress, anxiety and depression, the emotional and physical deterioration of aging.

In eulogizing ______________ ______________, it is fitting and appropriate to identify him as a "moisted" Jew. He was fresh and vigorous, vital and vibrant to the very end, because he was centered on goodness and rooted in Godliness. He had a very personal relationship with the Almighty and was one of the דבקים who clung to God all the days of his life, attending daily *minyan* and studying Torah daily. His eyes were not dimmed nor did freshness of body and spirit ever abate. He was bedewed and affused with faith and imbued with the refreshing "moisture" of Torah living.

Long ago, the prophet Isaiah observed:

וקׁוֵי ה׳ יחליפה כח יעלו אבר כנשרים ירוצו ולא ייגעו ילכו ולא ייעפו (ישעי׳ מ:לא)

"But they that wait for the Lord shall renew their strength;
They shall mount up with wings as eagles;
They shall run and not be weary;
They shall walk, and not faint" (Isaiah 40:31).

Isaiah's prophecy is a summary of ______________ ______________'s life. Moreover, commenting on the *pasuk,* ולא נס לֵחֹה "nor his natural force abated," the Talmud comments א״ר אליעזר בן יעקב, אל תקרא לא נס לחה אלא לא נס לֵחֹה עכשיו the blessings of ______________ ______________ belong not in the past, but reach into the future. For ______________ ______________ will continue to influence our lives for good, and his memory will inspire those who loved and admired him to emulate his example.

שלום לעפרו

"Too Soon to Cry"

לז״נ אמי מורתי הצנועה מאשא רבקה בת ר׳ משה ע״ה
Dedicated to the memory of my beloved mother

by Hershel Cohen

(For an active woman who died unexpectedly; for a woman
named Sarah; for *Parashat Ḥayei Sarah*)

ויבא אברהם לספד לשרה ולבכתה. (בראשית כג:ב) "And Abraham came
to mourn for Sarah, and weep for her" (Genesis 23:2).

It has long been pondered: why did the Torah place *hesped*,
"eulogy," before *bechiah*, "weeping." Human nature and common sense dictate the reverse order. The first reaction to bereavement is spontaneous, emotional, hysterical, fierce. It is a time for
weeping, not words. When the savage, violent emotions subside
and some measure of rational thinking returns, it is possible to
indulge in rhetoric, even eloquence.

There is one exception. When a vital, viable, active person
suddenly dies, repression and denial, those pervasive defenses,
conspire with shock and incredulity to reverse the order of events.
The family is too stunned by the unforeseen, unanticipated tragedy even for tears. They refuse to accept the tragic fact that their
beloved wife and mother is gone forever. Instinctively, they begin
to deal with the loss by describing the works and virtues of the
deceased. In their minds, she still lives. The *hesped* is not a eulogy
for the dead, but a *personality profile* of the one who, to the
mourners, is still a vital part of the family.

The death of Sarah was too sudden and surprising for Abraham to accept. He had just returned from the *akedah* on Mount
Moriah with Isaac alive and well. He could hardly wait to share
the joyous news with his wife. They could, at last, look forward to
years of happiness as an intact family secure in their faith in a

benevolent God who does *not* demand human sacrifice. The death of Sarah was like a dream—a nightmare—not real. He was too stunned to weep. Instead, he spoke about Sarah proudly, as if painting a beautiful word-picture, a keepsake for friends.

Our eyes, too, are not yet fully adjusted to the weeping mode, because those who knew and loved __________ __________ are not yet prepared to accept the bitter fact that this modern Sarah is no longer with us. But, the tears will come in due time, and we pray that they will elicit the consolation that what the family lost so precipitously they once had as their own, and that the beautiful memories she has bequeathed to them will be a cherished treasure to sustain them, this time for a future without end.

And after the tears will come the joyous realization that her most precious gift to them is the treasure of faith in God Almighty and faith eternal—and the belief in *life* triumphant.

שלום לעפרו

"A Fear for the Future"

ז״נ אחי ר׳ שמעון יוסף ב״ר אברהם אלחנן הלוי ת׳נ׳צ׳ב׳ה׳
Dedicated to the memory of my beloved brother
Samuel J. Solomon,

by Victor M. Solomon

(For a good person who died young)

א״ר לוי שבטים מציאה מצאו כתיב ״ויצא לבם״ ואנו שאבדו את ר׳ סימן עאכ״ו
(ב״ר, צ״א) "Rabbi Levi said: The tribes (i.e., Joseph's brothers)
found a lost article. It is written 'and their heart failed them.'
(Genesis 42:28) And we who have lost Rabbi Simon *a for-
tiori!*"

At first glance, to compare the discovery by Joseph's startled
brothers of the money in their sacks with the death of Rabbi
Simon appears far-fetched, if not absurd. In a deeper sense,
however, Rabbi Levi apparently registered the notion that the
death of a fine human being is more tragic than the immediate
subtraction of a person. It is a deficit for the future and a for-
feiture of wisdom, counsel and paradigm for generations unborn.

People tend to be jubilant when they find money. This was
not true of Joseph's brothers when they found the money in their
sacks. Why were they not glad but sad and frightened? Because
they suspected a trap, a ruse, a lure behind that fortune. They
feared Joseph, his stern rebuke and his accusation! The joy of the
moment was obscured by their fear of the future.

We are here not only to weep for a fine human being cut
down in his prime, but to mourn rejected hopes, negated wishes,
frustrated dreams, confuted expectations. It is the tragedy of an
unrealized potential, a future unfulfilled. Here is the ultimate
confrontation with the agonizing moment of truth concerning our
own mortality, our own vulnerability, and the abrupt annihilation

of innocent illusions. Thus, the loss of __________ __________ is a bereavement not only for the family, but also a very personal loss for everyone who knew and loved him. He will be missed— and we sense that vaster loss of an undefined potential, a future dimension for which we grieve even more.

Yet, even as the trepidation of Joseph's brethren diminished with time and was altogether nullifed by history, so may we, too, hope to find among us those who will continue in the path set forth by __________ __________ and potentiate his dreams as a living memorial, a meaningful future consecrated to a precious person.

May __________ __________'s family find solace in the gift of his brief but precious few years among us and in the good name he leaves behind.

שלום לעפרו

"The Third Name"

(For a popular person; one who endeared himself to the community; one who was known by endearing nicknames)

תני ג' שמות נקראו לאדם הזה. אחד שקראו לו אביו ואמו, ואחד שקראו לו
אחרים, ואחד שקראו לו בספר תולדותברייתו (מדרש קהלת רבתי, פרק ז':ג)

Each person, our Sages relate, is called by three names. The first is given by his parents. The second name is applied by the community. His third name is the one recorded in his personal chronicle. (Midrash Koheleth Ch. 7:3)

This Rabbinic observation merits more than the casual reflection often accorded ancient folklorist dicta. It reveals a deep philosophical view of man, the dynamic, optimistic percept of man's capacity to elevate himself above conventional horizontality, and to transcend conforming and confirming norms, forms, canons and apotheosized absolutes rendered obsolete by time.

During one's formative years one clings to the name given to him in infancy. With maturity, as a person confronts life, achieving professional success and recognition, the second name denoting career or calling comes to the fore. Both names are conferred by others. The third name sharply contrasts with the others, for it is the product of one's own elective decision. It is the name earned and selected through the nonverbal media of behavior, ingenuity, insight, foresight and service. In fact, posterity will remember him by the third name, *chosen by himself.*

______________ ____________ faithfully personifies this charming Rabbinic lesson in nomenclature. To his school buddies and childhood pals he was affectionately known as ___________. His associates and friends called him ___________.

In recent years, ___________ ____________ appeared on the scene as a champion of morality and ethics in government, an inspired defender of traditional Judaism, a staunch supporter of Torah and Torah institutions. He became active at Yeshiva University, identified with the Orthodox Union and tirelessly supported Israel through the Religious Zionists of America.

The future historian of the American Jewish community will unavoidably reckon with the name of ___________ ___________, his life and his dream. Indeed, his *third* name will be his enduring, endearing memorial.

שלום לעפרו

"Self-Made Man"

(For a self-made man who rose "from rags to riches;" for a man
named Joseph.)

ויקח משה את עצמות יוסף עמו כי השבע השביע את בני ישראל לאמר פקד
יפקד אלקים אתכם והעליתם את עצמותי מזה אתכם. (שמות י״ג:י״ט). "And
Moses took the bones of Joseph with him; for he had straitly
sworn the children of Israel, saying: 'God will surely
remember you; and ye shall carry up my bones away hence
with you'" (Exodus 13:19).

Moses, strikingly unlike vain leaders of victorious armies,
did not celebrate his historic triumph over Egypt and the liberation of his people from bondage with jubilation and patriotic
parades, but by fulfilling the wish of a dying man he had never
met. It was more than mere sentimentality. Moses wanted to
inscribe in the national consciousness of Israel the prescript of
Jewish eternity, for the bones of Joseph symbolize the intermina-
bility of Israel.

Joseph's life is the classic "success" story of a young lad who
rose from the humble status of a housekeeper in an Egyptian
nobleman's home to become the viceroy of Egypt, second only to
pharaoh himself. And Moses, the most faithful and loving leader
Israel ever had, wanted his people to have the inspiring image of
Joseph before their very eyes in that crucial moment of liberation.
How fitting that the Israelites who were celebrating their ascent
from slavery to freedom and their status of a "Kingdom of
Priests" should be cheered and encouraged in their new uncertain
role by the memory of Joseph who also rose "from rags to riches."

As we bid ___________ ___________ farewell we may, like,
Moses, challenge his beloved children to carry with them on the
road of life the beautiful memories of their father and his spectacular rise like Joseph, from a humble outset to a position of

respect and prominence in the business community. He had no formal education; when his friends attended school, he was compelled to support a widowed mother and orphaned siblings. In the end he became an advisor of celebrated artists and academicians. With his unique blend of practical ingenuity and stubborn determination, __________ __________ became a leader in his field and an example for others to follow. Yet, like Joseph, he did not forget his humble origins or reject his people. His commitments to synagogue, Federation, UJA and Israel grew with the years.

Your father's memory, like *Atzmot Yosef* will guide you in the years ahead. May it brighten your lives and bless your homes, and keep you ever mindful of the wonderful human qualities your father possessed—and bequeathed to the generations.

תהא נשמתו צרורה בצרור החיים

May his soul be bound up in the bond of life. Amen.

"The New Moon Jew"

(For a humble, fine, charitable person who preferred anonymity
and simplicity throughout his life; on Rosh Ḥodesh)

Innovation and change distinguish Sabbaths and festivals
from ordinary days of the week. Abstention from work, lighting
of candles, special foods and other marks of singularity set apart
days of special religious significance, giving them a unique
character.

One holiday in the Jewish calendar is the exception. Beyond
the walls of the synagogue where a few passages are added to the
services, it passes virtually unnoticed. There are no initiatory
rituals like *kiddush* to usher it in or a farewell service like *hav-
dalah* to bring it to a close, yet it is a very important festival. The
Torah numbers it among the major holidays with special offerings
and the sounding of the *shofar* (Numbers 10:10). In fact, the dates
of all the other holidays are determined by this neglected festival. I
am referring, of course, to *Rosh Ḥodesh*, a festival without external manifestation that celebrates the new month throughout the
year.

There are people whose personality commands attention,
who invite spectacular fame through outstanding personal
characteristics and charismatic factors. These may be called the
"Holiday Jews." There are others who in spite of their wisdom,
erudition, skills and dedication to worthy causes remain essential-
ly incognito. These are the "*Rosh Ḥodesh* Jews," those humble,
modest, shy, self-effacing people.

We have come here this day to pay our respects to one of the
latter. _________ _________ was a genuine "*Rosh Ḥodesh*
Jew." Unspoiled by success, unaware of his beautiful personhood,
unimpressed by his own sterling reputation, _________

__________ preferred the anonymity, humility and simplicity that distinguished his life and that he cultivated to a fault.

The passing of __________ __________ is a painful loss to all, and his absence will be felt in the community for a long time, for he was one of that nearly extinct species, those rare few "New Moon Jews" who work for the community *lishmah* and give of themselves to help others, seeking no reward or fame in exchange.

שלום לעפרו

(Based on a thought by my revered rebbe and master, the gaon Rabbi Joseph B. Soloveitchik).

"The Sanctuary of Public Service"

לז״נ אחי הקדוש שמואל ליב הכהן ז״ל שנספה בשנת השואה עם רעיתו וב״ב הי״ד
Dedicated to my dear brother who perished in the Nazi German
Holocaust together with his wife and children

by Hershel Cohen

(For an honest judge, lawyer, elected or appointed public official, or an uncorrupted man named Samuel)

הנני ענו בי נגד ה׳ ונגד משיחו את שור מי לקחתי וחמור מי לקחתי ואת מי עשקתי
את מי רצותי ומיד מי לקחתי כפר ואעלים עיני בו ואשיב לכם (שמואל א׳ י״ב:ג).
"Here I am; witness against me before the Lord, and before His
annointed: whose ox have I taken? or whose ass have I taken? or
whom have I defrauded? or whom have I oppressed? or of whose
hand have I taken a ransom to blind mine eyes therewith? and I
will restore it to you" (II Samuel 12:3).

The prophet Samuel had devoted his life to the Sanctuary and
had the stature of Moses and Aaron in the eyes of his people. At
the end of his days, when he wished to summarize the high point
of his life that might serve as an example for his people to follow,
he did not mention a word about his years devoted to the Temple
or his dedicated service in the House of the Lord.

What of his background did Samuel choose to spotlight in his
parting words to Israel? That he had clean hands. Having enjoyed
significant status that could have brought him material gain from
the public he served, Samuel had eschewed all selfish bounty and
did not covet personal gratuities during all the years of his
ministry.

This encomium belongs, also, to the deceased. ____________
___________ composed his own eulogy, not with words, but in the
idiom of a public servant who lived life honestly and was moti-
vated to strive not for personal gain but for the benefit of society.

In the company of the powerful at City Hall and on the exalted bench of the Superior Court, ___________ ___________ maintained scrupulously clean hands, a pure heart and a clear conscience.

Others, like Samuel, may have spent more time in sanctuaries and houses of worship. ___________ ___________, also like Samuel, dedicated his life to sanctifying society, perfecting people and ministering to mankind by administering justice. And above all, he served God devotedly by bringing harmony into the lives of men and tranquility into the domestic affairs of husbands and wives and families. For the name of God is "Peace."

שלום לעפרו

"A Woman's Place"

(For a pious, active woman who devoted her life to the community; a woman who asserted her right to a significant place
in the community; *Sidrot Shelaḥ* and *Pinḥas*)

א״ר חסדא מ״ט דכתיב ״ויבן ה׳ אלקים את הצלע . . . מלמד שנתן הקב״ה בינה
יתירה באשה יותר מבאיש (נדה מ״ה:ע״ב). "R. Ḥisda stated: What is
Rabbi's reason? Because it is written in Scripture, 'And the Lord
God built (*wayiben*) the rib' (Genesis 2:22) which teaches that the
Holy One, blessed be He, endowed the woman with more understanding (i.e., *binah*, of a root that is analogous to that of *wayiben*) than man" (Nidah 45b).

תנה לנו אחזה בתוך אחי אבינו (במדבר כ״ז:ד). "Give (*t'nah*) unto us a
possession among the brethren of our father" (Numbers 27:4).

נתנה ראש ונשובה מצרימה (שם יד:ד). "Let us make (*nitnah*) a captain,
and let us return to Egypt" (Ibid. 14:4).

*   *   *   *   *

There is an egregiously distorted notion among some Jewishly
marginal "activists" that Jewish tradition confines women to the
home and consigns them to the imperspicuous and inelegant roles
of mother and kitchen personnel. Jewish history eloquently belies
this canard. The Miriams, Abigails, Deborahs, Hannahs, Beru-
riahs, Huldas and uncounted myriads of *nashim tzidkaniot*,
Jewish heroines, the acknowledged guarantors of Jewish survival
and liberation, testify to the majestic role Judaism bestowed on its
"women of valor."

——————— ———————, inspired by this noble heritage, lived
a life of dedication and service to God and His children. Like the
daughters of Zelophehad, she yearned for and earned a place of
dignity and communal recognition among the Children of Israel.
Indeed, she won the highest respect of everyone for her brilliance
and insight as much as for her service and dedication.

It is noteworthy that the Torah, according to Rabbinic tradition, awarded the greatest honor to women. Rabbi Ḥisda observed that women were endowed by God with a special measure of wisdom not given to men. Moreover, when men said *nitnah* and were prepared to abandon their objectives and return to Egypt, the women saved the day by insisting with the daughters of Zelophehad on *t'nah* i.e., "give us a possession among our father's brethren—let us remain faithful to our goals.

_____________ _____________ was a worthy daughter of Zelophehad, faithful to the God of her parents, devoted to her husband and children, dedicated to our congregation and a genuine source of encouragement to the Jewish community, which, in difficult moments, resorted to the *nitnah* philosophy of defeatist pessimism. _____________ _____________ always counseled *t'nah*, and she earned her spiritual "possession" among the daughters of Zelophehad and the countless heroines of Jewish history.

תהא נשמתה צרורה בצרור החיים

May her soul be bound up in the bond of the living. Amen.

"In the Company of Hashem*"*

(For a charitable person who died childless; for a person
named Moses, Aaron, Miriam, Elazar)

בשעת פטירתו של אהרון אמר לו משה, אהרון אחי, ראה מרים מתה, אני ואתה
טפלנו בה. אתה מת, אני ואלעזר מטפלים בך. ואני, אם מת אני, מי מטפל בי? אמר לו
הקב״ה למשה, חייך אני מטפל בך (ילקוט שמעוני פ׳ חקת). "When Aaron was
dying, Moses said to him, 'Aaron my brother, see, when Miriam
died I and you tended to her. When you die, I and Elazar are tending to you. As for me, when I die who will tend to me?' Where-
upon the Holy One blessed be he said to Moses, 'I swear that I
will tend to you'" (*Yalkut Shimoni, Parashat Ḥukat*).

Perhaps the most pervasive universal wish is that, in the final
act when the curtain comes down on the drama of life, the end
should come with grace and dignity. The children most often
strive to accomplish this in compliance with the expressed wishes
of a parent. Since not all people are blessed with children, the
"Golden Years" of such hapless individuals tend to be marked by
concern about their final days. Preoccupation concerning the last
rites and the propriety of the closing chapter of their lives can give
rise to intense worry and genuine anxiety for ordinary people.

How strange that Moses, the incomparable leader and law-
giver, should find himself in such a tragic predicament! When
Moses was called by *Hashem* to redeem His people from slavery,
he invested himself totally in the service of the Lord, ignoring all
personal concerns, including his family. All that mattered to him
was the perfect fulfillment of his obligation and role as משה עבדו—
Moses His servant.

Ministering to his dying brother, Moses felt overwhelmed by
the enormity of his own tragedy, a devastating loneliness compounded by a practical concern for his own eventual end when
none of his contemporaries would remain to minister to his final

needs and obsequies. *Hashem* assured him that *He* would be there!

In this solemn moment consecrated to the memory of __________ ______________, we, too, can affirm sincerely that *Hashem* will do no less for __________ ____________ than He did for Moses. *Hashem*, Himself, so to speak, will serve on his *Ḥevra Kadisha*. For __________ ____________ has left a large family, not of flesh and blood, but of heart and soul. The countless beneficiaries of his generosity will truly mourn for him and proclaim in their hearts: צדק לפניו יהלך, ''Righteousness shall go before him (Psalms 85:14).

The wife and family will derive much comfort from the kind of life he lived and the belief that __________ ____________ is now in the company of *Hashem*.

שלום לעפרו

"When Words Fail: Tears"

(For the youthful victim of a very tragic accident, or when several family members lose their lives in a mishap)

רבי שמעון בן אלעזר אומר: אל תרצה את חברך בשעת כעסו ואל תנחמהו בשעה שמתו מוטל לפניו, וכו' (אבות פ"ד:כ"ג) "Rabbi Shimon ben Elazar says: Do not appease your fellow in the time of his anger; do not console him while his dead lies before him, etc." (Avoth, Ch. 4, *Mishnah* 23).

While the difference between the physical and spiritual realms is quite clear in that the former occupies space and the latter does not, yet, in one respect they are patently alike, for even the mind and heart can be filled with emotions and impressions. At times, sentiments can be so powerful as to prevent the penetration of other words and feelings. Just as an exceptionally powerful man is needed to remove a very heavy physical object, only an extraordinary affect must be applied to neutralize an overwhelming thought or emotion.

This can explain Rabbi Shimon ben Elazar's dictum, "Do not console him while his dead lies before him." At that time, the mind and heart are so overwhelmed by acute grief that reasonable words of consolation and rational expressions of comfort are of marginal value to the bereaved. Well-intentioned verbiage can be irritating if not entirely disturbing, and may leave the perplexed consoler painfully frustrated.

Tragedy is often unreasonable. In this instance, it is also beyond words. The anguish of the __________ family is so deep and excruciating that no eulogy could assuage the pain in mind and heart. In truth, we are here not to console, but to join you in weeping—to mingle our tears with yours as we recall the beautiful life of __________ __________ cut so tragically and needlessly short.

A wonderful legend about a comforting cup comes to mind. God, so the tender story goes, holds a כוס דמעות, a cup in which He collects the tears shed by our people throughout the centuries of suffering and exile. When the cup of tears is filled, we are assured, the Messiah will come and redeem the world.

When words fail, tears unite and console. The copious tears of this noble family and of all of us here to share in this tragic moment will surely add to the כוס דמעות and hasten the coming of the Messiah when God Himself will dry all tears, vanquish death and restore life everlasting to His loved ones.

בלע המות לנצח ומחה ה׳ דמעה מעל כל פנים

"A Different Drummer"

(For an atheist, agnostic, nonobservant or nonpracticing Jew whose philanthropic inclination and respect for Jewish values were derived from a religious education in his youth)

רוכב הייתי על הסוס ומטייל אחורי בית המקדש ביום הכפורים שחל להיות בשבת
ושמעתי בת קול מצפצפת ואומרת שובו בנים שובבים שובו אלי ואשובה אליכם חוץ
מאלישע בן אבויה שהיה יודע כחי ומרד בי (מדרש קהלת ז:י"ח)

Many who have strayed from the Jewish path and abandoned Torah experience moments of nostalgia for the faith of their parents, and sense occasional stirrings of religious sensitivity, if not ecstacy. Such feelings could be activated by "time" and "place."

The temporal factor is a Shabbat potential every week. All week long, a person is absorbed in his career or profession, distracted by the pervasive dynamics of acculturation, assimilation and erosion of religious principles. Comes Shabbat, and recovery occurs as he recalls his roots and childhood memories. He longs to return.

The spatial factor could eventuate on passing a synagogue, *beth midrash* or *yeshiva*. A gentle tug at the Jewish heartstrings, and he yearns to return. If these factors fail to move him, Yom Kippur will certainly exert the desired influence on the recalcitrant renegade.

Elisha ben Avuya was so estranged from his faith and the Jewish nurture of his youth that neither the "time" of Shabbat nor the "place" of the Temple—and not even Yom Kippur—had any impact on his attitude toward the faith of his parents. Yet, the name of Elisha ben Avuya is mentioned among the venerable Sages of the Mishnah in Tractate *Avoth, Ethics of the Fathers.* Why? Because Jewish tradition accepted the liberal view of his disciple, Rabbi Meir, to extract the nutritious kernel and discard the shell.

————————— ————————— was a fine human being, though estranged from his faith, who marched to the beat of a different drummer. He had his own philosophy of life. His faith was a humanistic system of justice, integrity, fairness in interpersonal matters and a sense of concern for his fellowmen. Neither Shabbat nor synagogue—not even Yom Kippur—moved him to return to the path of Torah that he had studied in his younger years. He believed that feeding the hungry was more important than fasting on Yom Kippur, speaking kindly to people accomplished more than praying to God, and working for peace was more significant than resting on Shabbat.

Though we know that ethics without Torah can be perverted and certainly will not long endure, and that there is more to Judaism than humanistic ideals, we are constrained by Jewish tradition to respect ————————— ————————— for his ethical views and to mourn his passing because of his many good deeds that benefitted people and charitable institutions. We dare not do less for ————————— ————————— than what our Sages did for Elisha ben Avuya.

שלום לעפרו

"A Swimming Champion: Jewish Style"

(For a *Ḥozer Bit'shuva*, an estranged Jew who reaffirmed his
Jewish identity)

מה רב טובך אשר צפנת ליראיך פעלת לחוסים בך נגד בני אדם (תהלים ל"א:כ)
"Oh how abundant is Thy goodness, which Thou hast laid up for
them that fear Thee; Which Thou hast wrought for them that
take their refuge in Thee, in sight of the sons of man!" (Psalms
31:20)

The Chofetz Chaim observed that swimming with the current
is no true measure of an athlete's prowess. One who can swim
against the current displays the athletic acumen of a champion.
Similarly, the person who breaks away from the popular trends of
the times and decides to set his life on a new and socially defiant
personal course in the direction of maximal Jewish identity and
Torah loyalty has the characteristics of a spiritual hero, one who
has the resourcefulness of soul to go נגד בני אדם.

__________ __________ was such a person. A eulogy is, by
definition, a tribute to the deceased. In this instance there is very
little tribute to bestow on __________ __________, for the better
part of his lifetime was not devoted to spiritual matters. In fact,
there was nothing religiously significant about the early decades
of his life. __________ __________ was born into a marginal
Jewish family with little, if any, interest in Jews and Judaism. He
learned from his parents to maintain a low Jewish profile, and he
followed through by avoiding any contact with Jews except when
absolutely necessary in business. During that phase of his life
__________ __________, like most people, swam *with* the stream.

Suddenly, __________ __________ changed direction. It was a
momentous decision when he elected to join a synagogue and affiliate with the Jewish Federation as an active member. Next came
tefillin, *kashruth*, *Sabbath* observance, and a life dedicated to
Torah and *mitzvot*. While acculturation and assimilation were

decimating American Jewry, _____________ _____________ discovered the mystical beauty in Judaism and lovingly embraced it. Indeed, he witnessed through his newly acquired lifestyle to the relevancy of a dedicated Jewish life for the contemporary American intellectual. _____________ _____________ was a champion of the spirit, a genuine hero. Convinced that the direction of his life had been wrong, he summoned enough daring and tenacity to make a U-turn in midstream and to swim courageously *against the current.*

We bow our heads reverently in the presence of so valiant a man, and pray that many others will choose his path, seek his goals and find the deep satisfaction that _____________ _____________ discovered in his faith.

צדיק באמונתו יחי'

The *tzadik* shall find eternal life in his faith.

"Disagreeing Agreeably"

(For a homosexual who died of AIDS, a sinner, an irreligious
Jew, or a nonobservant Jew)

(ברכות ח:) לוחות ושברי לוחות מונחות בארון ''The Tablets and the
broken fragments of the Tablets were placed in the (same) box''
(Berakhot, 8b).

The story of the Golden Calf apostacy, the consequent broken
Tablets of the Law and the preparation of a second set of Tablets
by Moses reflects the sequence of events in many a person's life.
In our youth, we tend to accept faith in God and His precepts with
enthusiasm like the ancient Israelites who, in the early years of a
young nation, exuberantly proclaimed נעשה ונשמע, we shall do
even before we shall understand!

With adolescence come skepticism and doubt. Faith is ques-
tioned, religious regulations critiqued, and Torah and tradition are
tested. It is a stage of life devoted to ''Tablet breaking.'' Some of
these rebellious teenagers eventually return to God. Others
remain divorced from His way forever, devoting themselves to a
life of good deeds and noble actions—stripped of any religious
meaning.

The Rabbis tell us that the broken Tablets were not discarded.
Even the shattered pieces were infused with a measure of significant sanctity. Thus, Moses placed those pieces alongside the new,
whole Tablets of the Law. It was ordained that the broken fragments rest side by side, in one and the same box.

Today we pay our last respects to ________ _________, a
man who, to some degree, broke the Tablets of Jewish Law. He
sincerely believed that one could live a lifestyle at variance with
the Torah concept of morality and propriety and still be a decent,
good and loving human being.

It is religiously right and in good taste, from the Jewish perspective, to respect his convictions lovingly, while disagreeing

with them passionately, and honoring his right to his own view of life without endorsing it. In doing so we emulate *Moshe Rabbeinu*, Moses, who taught us that the broken fragments belong alongside the new whole Tablets in the same box.

______________ ______________ did many beautiful and noble things that some men of religion rarely consider worthy of their time. He was especially concerned about the environment—i.e., God's earth. He tried to protect it from abuse in his own way. He was active in the humane society and tried to implement the Jewish concern for animal welfare (*tza'ar ba'aley chayim*) by caring for God's creatures. He also cared for his fellowmen regardless of creed or ethnic or racial identification, like God who created and sustains a multiplex and multifaceted universe and family of man.

______________ ______________ was, above all, an extraordinarily *kind human being.*

May these beautiful virtues accompany ______________ ______________ to the Heavenly Throne and may his *kindness* be an eternal monument to honor his memory among us.

שלום לעפרו

"With God's Approval"

(For a divorcee or a bachelor; one named Moses or Simeon)

שלשה דברים עשה משה מדעתו והסכים הקב"ה עמו. הוסיף יום אחד מדעתו ופירש מן האשה ושבר את הלוחות (שבת פ"ז:ע"א) ''Three things did Moses do of his own understanding, and the Holy One, blessed be He, gave His approval: he added one day of his own understanding, he separated himself from his wife, and he broke the Tables'' (Shabbat, 87a).

Part of the human predicament is that there is within people a constant state of conflict. Man strives to attain an individuated and distinct personality. He seeks recognition as a special individual with a unique character. On the other hand, man is also a part of the human family, with many communal obligations and societal expectations. He is expected to get married, build a home, raise a family, and pursue a career. The greater the person, the more intense the conflict.

Some of the most illustrious historical personalities, including Judah Maccabeus and Kant, gave up marriage in favor of intellectual pursuits, idealism and social service. They believed that they could better serve mankind undistracted by and unencumbered with marital and cognate obligations. Even Shimon ben Azai, the great Talmudic sage, eschewed nuptial joy, finding his fulfillment in Torah, and remained a bachelor all his life.

Criticism of such individuals is at one's peril, and should be done with care and circumspection, for their ranks include an array of noble heroes of the world and the spirit who have profoundly influenced our lives. Even Moses, the greatest prophet of all time, saw fit at one point in his life to separate from his wife because the significance of his historic spiritual mission transcended the legitimate demands of marriage and family and connubial obligations—and God agreed with him!

__________ __________, whom we have come to bid farewell and to eulogize today, belongs to that select group of dedicated individuals who chose to serve the Jewish community selflessly and in a way divergent from the common ideal, but deeply rooted in a noble tradition. It is for us to honor his decision and to admire his sacrifice, even as God assented to the choice of Moses.

__________ __________ had a special sense of pride in his Jewish identity and served the Jewish community with sacrificial devotion. His name and achievements will long be remembered by all of us, his spiritual heirs, who have become his grieving family. In our midst __________ __________ has achieved immortality.

שלום לעפרו

Grape Jews

ז״נ חתני הרה״ג ר׳ צבי הירש ב״ר יוסף הכהן
Dedicated to the Memory of My Beloved Sainted and Revered
Father-in-Law and Friend, Rabbi Hershel Cohen
By Victor M. Solomon

(For a kind, loving, honest, friendly person)

Rabbi Hayim Vital, the noted 16th century Cabalist, observed in his celebrated esoteric tome *Aitz HaḤayim*, that all fruits can be classified in three categories. First, there are the hard-shelled fruits and nuts, like the coconut, whose delicious interior awaits the perservering soul undeterred by the unyielding, tough exterior. The second group are the delectable fruits, like peaches and plums, that are soft and ready to eat, but contain a hard pit at the core. The third genre of fruit are delightfully soft throughout, neither tough shell without nor hard pit within causing grief to the diner. The grape belongs to this phylum.

Human beings, according to Rabbi Vital, can also be thus classified. There are people who appear cold, hard and withdrawn. Yet, when you get to know them, you will find in them a warm heart and a kind soul. These are the coconut type. Others impress you with all manner of external virtues. They are gregarious, outgoing and involved. However, on an intimate level you discover the hard pit, a selfish, self-centered core which is usually kept discreetly concealed by the peach or plum people. Those who are compassionate, loving, sincere and honest within and without, at every level and at all times, belong to the *grape* family. When the prophet spoke affectionately of the Jews, he compared them to the grape: כענבים במדבר מצאתי את ישראל (הושע ט׳:י׳). ''I found Israel like grapes in the desert'' (Hosea 9:10).

____________ ____________ to whom we pay our last respects today, belonged unreservedly to that singular company of Grape Jews. Warm, tender, friendly and kind at all times and at every level of relationship, ____________ ____________ cultivated in the desert of contemporary society an oasis of compassion, kindness and human concern.

____________ ____________'s family may find comfort in the awareness that they were blessed with a unique husband and father whose life was so rich in virtues and sublime gifts. The community, too, lost one of its noblest sons.

May his life ennoble us all and remind us always that we can also aspire to the highest classification of man and transmute the social desert around us into a vineyard of love.

שלום לעפרו

(For some mysterious reason, *Grape Jews* was my sainted father-in-law's favorite eulogette.)

BOOK TWO

UNVEILINGS — הקמת מצבות

„ונטה את שפרירו עליהם" (ירמי׳ מ״ג:י׳)
''He shall spread his royal pavilion over them'' (Jeremiah 43:10)

"Tribute to a Man of God"

(For a person who combined religious commitment with ethical
and loving behavior)

ויאמר מה הציון הלז אשר אני רואה? ויאמרו אליו אנשי העיר הקבר איש
האלקים אשר בא מיהודה

King Josiah said, "What kind of a monument is that which I
see? The men of the city said to him: it is the grave of a man of
God who came from Judah" (II Kings 23:17).

The title "man of God" implies a harmonious blending of
heavenly and earthly qualities. Every person is a combination of
the physical and the spiritual.

מפלגא ולתתא איש, ומפלגא למעלה אלקים—"from the waist down,
man; from the waist up, angel." It is a grievous error to neglect
either one of these vital components. "A man of God," therefore,
is one who combines in his mode of living these two attributes,
the heavenly and the earthly.

Should someone ask, *Mah hatziyun halaz?*—"what kind of
monument are we about to unveil?" the answer would be: "It is
the grave of a *man of God*, a man who lived both parts to the fullest. He combined work and prayer. He served his Creator with
heart and soul, but he also served his fellowman selflessly, without interest in personal reward. This monument is a memorial to a
true *man of God*."

"A Living Tablet"

(For a person who devoted his life to promote Jewish education and Torah study)

We are assembled here to remember a person who left a bereaved family and a disconsolate community, and to dedicate a memorial stone inscribed with his name. The Hebrew term for this ceremony, הקמת מצבה, denotes the placing of a stone marker on the grave and connotes the unveiling of a stone monument. The engraved words reflect the essence and significance of the service.

Why all this attention and honor accorded a מצבה, a simple stone, when Judaism, throughout our history, has consistently favored matters of the spiritual, the sacred and the ethical over the materialistic? Our ancestors were content to leave the building of pyramids, parthenons and assorted wonders of brick and stone to others. Indeed, the pretext and the context of this unveiling ceremony is not the stone, but the text itself, the inscription *on* the monument. By reading the lines of that inscription we learn the life story of the one to whom it is dedicated. Once again, we become aware of the irreparable loss sustained by the family and the community.

From a metaphysical perspective, each one of us is, in fact, a mere דומם, an inanimate collection of dust particles molded into the configuration of a human being. However, this inanimate and lifeless form is inspired and suffused with a spirit, a soul, a living tablet inscribed with eloquent lines consecrated to noble deeds and precious dreams, words that relate a story of life. One whose life-lines deserve to tell a story worthy of public commendation is respected during his lifetime and continues to be honored after he is called to his heavenly rest.

We are gathered here today for a service that transcends the unveiling of a mere monument of stone. Our purpose is to unveil the inspiring life story of ___________ ___________, graceful lines reflecting noble deeds and beautiful dreams. Unfortunately, no monument is large enough for the entire story of his life, the many causes for which he gave unselfishly of his time and effort, the institutions he supported, his love of Torah, Israel and the Jewish people, his devotion to family and friends.

The many wonderful life-lines inscribed on his living, vibrant monument by his lifestyle of Torah and Torah standards are a tribute to him and a challenge for us. If we declare this ground sacred, it is only by virtue of the sanctification he has already bestowed on it by his presence.

Let the monument serve as a symbol and a reminder to all those who pass by that here rests ___________ ___________ who inscribed a living memorial with lines from a life nobly lived, and sanctified a stone with everlasting value and grace.

תהא נשמתו צרורה בצרור החיים

"A Lesson in Living—From Tombstones"

(For a virtuous person who was charitable and "genuine")

שבשעת פטירתו של אדם אין מלוים לו לאדם לא כסף ולא זהב ולא אבנים טובות ומרגליות אלא תורה ומעשים טובים בלבד. (אבות ו:ט) "In the hour of one's departure neither silver nor gold nor precious stones nor pearls accompany him, but only Torah and good works. . . ." (Avoth 6:9)

As we look about us at the monuments in the cemetery, we notice a pervasive homogeneity of text and sentiment. The striking similitude is more than coincidental. The inscriptions invariably declare that the deceased was a paragon of virtues, a very righteous person who devoted his life to God and fellowman. If we were but marginally aware of man's frailty and fallibility, we would be forgiven our incredulous, if not outright cynical, assessment of these ubiquitous panegyrics and stereotyped, undifferentiated acclamations. Were they all really such spiritual heroes, as noble and righteous and pious as the texts would have us believe?

Of course not! They were human beings and few who qualify as such can lay claim to moral perfection and ethical rectitude. People are people, and people are an amalgam of good and evil, love and hate, mercy and cruelty, spiritual grandeur and crass materialism. The *Yetzer Tov* and the *Yetzer Hara*, those two primeval antagonists, are still locked in mortal combat within every man's heart. Then why all the cheers and adulations?

This is a very important lesson on the meaning of life. The inscriptions are meant to inform us that not everything we do during our lifetime is worth remembering. In fact, many of the most desirable achievements on earth are best forgotten in the sobering atmosphere of a *beit olam*, the eternal resting place. Only that which is noble and righteous and pious is worth inscribing on stone for future generations to recall. Indeed, as we walk among the graves, we would be well advised to learn from these inscriptions what really counts in the context of eternal considerations so that we could take along with us into the *Artzot HaḤayim*, the Land of the Living, a blueprint of life worth following with inner satisfaction and pride.

Your father (mother), whose monument we have just unveiled, is one of those rare individuals who religiously adhered to that blueprint. If this monument were without lines of adjectives, with only the name of the deceased inscribed, we could still read an impressive list of *authentic* virtues that were a palpable part of his (her) meaningful life. While there are lines that declare his (her) spiritual nobility, it is our duty to attest and witness that every word is true and genuinely deserved. In his (her) love of and support for Torah and practical devotion to Israel, he (she) is, indeed, without analogue and peer.

תהא נשמתו (נשמתה) צרורה בצרור החיים

May his (her) soul be bound up in the bond of life—and may his (her) memory ever inspire us to noble giving and consecrated living. Amen.

"The Real Monument"

(For a kind and noble woman who supported philanthropic institutions and gave selflessly to help others; a woman named
Rachel; for *Parashat Vayishlaḥ*)

"And .ויצב יעקב מצבה על קברתה היא מצבת קברת רחל עד היום (בראשית ל"ה:כ)
Jacob set up a pillar upon her grave; the same is the pillar of
Rachel's grave unto this day" (Genesis 35:20).

At first glance the phrase היא מצבת קברת רחל, "the same is the
pillar (or monument) of Rachel's grave," seems redundant and
unessential. However, a closer look at these words reveals an
astoundingly significant message.

Most *matzeivot* or monuments are placed on the gravesite by
family members who wish to perpetuate the memory of a loved
one. Occasionally, the monument is prepared for herself by a far-
sighted person who plans ahead during her lifetime. She com-
poses her own epitaph or selects an appropriate one from a book
of poetry. When she passes on to her eternal reward, *her* monument, the one *she* prepared with the epitaph *she* composed or
selected is placed on her gravesite to tell the story of her life the
way *she* wanted it told.

Our Matriarch Rachel was such a woman. She prepared a
monument of love and devotion during her lifetime, inscribing it
with matchless deeds of faith in God, love for husband and children and devotion to her sister Leah. Indeed, when Jacob came to
mark the gravesite with a monument, ויצב יעקב מצבה על קברתה, he
found היא מצבת קברת רחל, that a *matzeivah* was already in place. היא,
i.e., *Rachel herself* was the monument; her beaufitul life was the
most eloquent epitaph, the finest tribute to her memory.

_____________ _____________, like Rachel, spent a lifetime preparing for this matchless moment. She composed her own eulogy not
of mere words, but of boundless love, faith and *mitzvot*. This

places us in a somewhat awkward predicament. Here we are about to consecrate this monument, supposedly provided by her husband and children, when, in fact, it is another monument that should be unveiled, the magnificent, though invisible, *matzeivah* ___________ ___________ prepared and inscribed with the graphic epitaph of her beautiful life, reflecting the joy of orphaned children she helped, flourishing *yeshivot* and other philanthropic institutions she supported, and the countless troubled souls, no longer troubled because she sustained them with a kind word and a contagious smile. היא the beautiful life of ___________ ___________, מצבת קברת רחל is the *matzeivah*, the *real* monument עד היום we unveil and consecrate to her everlasting memory today.

תהא נשמתה צרורה בצרור החיים

May the soul of ___________ ___________ be bound up in the bond of the living.

"Darkness Unto Light"

(General theme)

Tragedy and suffering can be utilized for personal refinement. The stars are visible only at night. Darkness increases human perception. Bereavement, which taxes a person's faith, also has the capacity to perfect it. Job, Rabbi Akiba and countless martyrs have affirmed this fact with their very lives.

The Midrash alludes to this fact in the following statement: א״ר חנינא: אמר הקב״ה עינים יש בתוכן לבן ושחור ואין אתה רואה מתוך הלבן אלא מתוך השחור (במדבר רבה) "Rabbi Chanina said: The Holy One blessed be He said: The eyes are composed of white and dark parts (Iris). One can see only through the dark part."

BOOK THREE

DIVREI TORAH — דברי תורה

TORAH DISCOURSES
FOR A HOUSE OF MOURNING
DURING SHIVA

„קל מסתתר בשפריר חביון" (זמירות לסעודה שלישית בשבת, יסדו וחברו ר׳ אברהם
מימין, תלמיד של ר׳ משה קורדיברו)
''God indwells in the hidden sanctuary'' (From the Table Hymn
assigned to the third meal on Shabbat, composed by Rabbi Abraham Maimin, disciple of Rabbi Moses Cordevero).

Kaddish:
Consoling God

(A *d'var Torah* for the week of *shiva*)

The *Kaddish*, as we know, makes no reference to death or the Hereafter. A charming interpretation of this popular and universally respected prayer (technically known as a ''doxology'') recited by mourners would, therefore, be welcome.

The Talmud (Tractate Berakhot, 49b) discusses the laws pertaining to *Birkhat Hamazon*, Grace After Meals, and the multiplex formulation of *zimun*, the ''Call to Say Grace:''

כיצד מזמנין? בשלשה אומר נברך . . . בעשרה אומר נברך אלקינו . . . במאה הוא אומר נברך ה׳ אלקינו . . . ובאלף הוא אומר נברך לה׳ אלקינו אלקי ישראל . . . ברבוא אומר נברך לה׳ אלקינו אלקי ישראל אלקי צבאות יושב בכרובים על המזון שאכלנו (ברכות מ״ט, ע״ב).

''When three dine together, they say 'With (your) consent, *let us bless* (the Lord).' When ten dine together, they add, 'Let us bless *our God.*' When 100 feast together, they add, 'Let us bless *the Lord our God.*' In the presence of a thousand banquetting together, we add, 'Let us bless the Lord our God, *the God of Israel.*' When 10,000 are at the banquet, we add, 'Let us bless the Lord our God, the God of Israel, *the Lord of Hosts who dwells at the Cherubim.*''''

The pattern of these configurations of the ''Call to Say Grace'' mandated by our Sages follows ascending, incremental levels of *kedushah* with increasing numbers of diners and, obversely, descending, decremental degrees of sanctity as the number of participants diminishes. *Zimun* does not even apply to a lone diner, while three who do ''Call to Say Grace'' do so without the name of the Lord. The ''Call to Say Grace'' in His Name is valid only in the presence of a minimum quorum of ten.

When a person is taken from this world the family and the community sustain a grievous loss. However, the demise of a human being constitutes an even greater and more tragic loss for the Almighty because His *kedushah* is determined by the number of faithful who praise Him and glorify His name. The loss of a single human being diminishes His degree of sanctity—for it is the living, not the dead, who hallow the name of God.

Here is where *kaddish* becomes a vital instrument in the intimate, exclusive and singular, if esoteric, relationship between God and His people Israel. God is, as it were, bereaved and grief-stricken by the loss of even one of His children. Thus, the son who comes to synagogue to say *kaddish* does so, in a metaphysical sense, to comfort God! With the *kaddish*, he consoles the Almighty: "My father (or mother), dear God, is no longer able to sanctify your name with prayer and praise. However, I am here to take his (or her) place. I shall continue to sanctify You even as father (or mother) did." The deceased will then be able to say, in the words of the psalmist, לא אמות כי אחיה "I shall *not* die, but live . . ." (Psalms 118:17) because the children, through their conduct, have provided their parents with posthumous life and eloquence. God, too, will be comforted by the assurance of orphans that His glory will not be diminished; the children have stepped into the ranks once occupied by the parents and will continue to sanctify His name.

"Reason to Believe"

(For sermons on faith, belief, hope, miracles, resurrection of the
dead, alienation)

Victor M. Solomon, Ch, Col, USAFR

Why Ezekiel's prophecy of the Valley of Dry Bones on the
Intermediate Sabbath (*Sabbath Ḥol Hamoed*) of Passover? *Rashi*
explains that according to one opinion, the dry bones belonged to
the Ephraimites who anticipated the Exodus by thirty years and
were killed in the wilderness. This vision is therefore topical on
Passover. Rashi and Radak interpret this passage as a statement of
faith in the Jewish mystery of survival against the laws of survival, and an affirmation of belief in an ultimate Redemption in
spite of an ostensibly endless exile. Hence, the selection of this
vision for public reading during *Pesach*. Rabbi Hai Gaon, quoted
by *Nimukei Yosef* on *Megillah*, attributes the choice of this passage as a Passover *Haftarah* to a tradition that resurrection will
take place in the month of Nissan.

Modern man has paid too high a spiritual price for admission
into the world of technology, exchanging faith for facts. What did
he gain by flying higher than a bird and probing the oceans deeper than a fish, if he forgot to walk upon the face of the earth like a
decent human being, the "Son of Man," if you will?

Man has lost the formula for faith, the capacity to believe. He
is often ashamed of his spiritual heritage, too embarrassed to
acknowlege an intrinsic need to commune with his Creator. So he
denies Him, and, like Adam, hides from God behind social, psy-
chological and political rationalizations, creeds and philosophies
designed to offer ersatz oblique spiritual relief and surcease from
the quagmire of alienation into which he has strayed.

Ezekiel's prophecy is a challenge to believe and a call to faith. Be not like the Ephraimites who jumped the gun and left Egypt thirty years before the Exodus, only to become a Valley of Dry Bones. Let God's word guide you as you seek your own emancipation. And if you will believe, test your faith on the doctrine of resurrection, for there are many who glibly acknowledge God the Creator who somehow falter when they come to God the "Re-Creator." And if your faith needs first aid, then consider the miracle of redemption and the mystery of Jewish survival, God's assurance that, for His children, the miraculous is standard, routine and commonplace.

BOOK FOUR

ELEGIAC SPARKS

From the Five Books of Moses Arranged by Sidrot

נפתלי אילה שלחה הנתן אמרי שפר (בראשית מ״ט:כ״א)
''Naphtali is a hind let loose, He giveth goodly words'' (Genesis
49:21)

From עת ספוד (*Et S'fod*)
by Rabbi S. Klein

A. בראשית — GENESIS

1. פ׳ בראשית: BEREISHIT

"And God saw every thing that He had made, and, behold, it was very good" (Genesis 1:31).
Our Sages explained that the word "very" alludes to "death."
When one lives a blameless life, then death is a mere continuation of that pure existence.

* * * * *

"And there was evening and there was morning, one day" (Genesis 1:5).
The mourner would find comfort in perceiving that both light and darkness coexist in one perfect day.

2. פ׳ נח: NOAH

Even as the rainbow (Genesis 9:13) signified the end of the deluge, so must people seek the hidden bright colors of consolation in every tragedy.

* * * * *

"I have set My bow in the cloud" (Genesis 9:13).
Just as the rainbow marks the end of the deluge, so have our Sages set limits to grief. Even mourning must end at some point in time.

3. פ׳ לך לך: LEKH LEKHA

"Get thee out of thy country" (Genesis 12:1).
Rashi comments: "For your own good." (Ibid) When a person must leave the "land of the living" there is much grief. However,

there can also be consolation if we could trust that one leaves for a good destination, i.e., a better world. Commenting on this verse, our Sages observed that genuine joy is reserved for the Hereafter. However, the loss of a child is too painful to bear unless one can truly believe that the child enjoys everlasting goodness in the Hereafter. The psalmist explains it in his own way:
"Give the king Thy judgments, O God,
And Thy righteousness unto the king's son" (Psalms 72:1), i.e., would that the father be judged by God as long as His mercy is on the son.

* * * * *

"And the king of Sodom said unto Abram: 'Give me the persons and take the goods to thyself'" (Genesis 14:21).
The angel of death surely spoke thus to the deceased: "Give me your soul; your spiritual goods of charitable acts and kind deeds will remain as an eternal monument."

4. פ׳ וירא: VAYEIRA

"And the men rose up from thence, and looked out toward Sodom" (Genesis 18:16).
Upon leaving the house of Abraham, the Angels viewed Sodom and apprehended the great spiritual gap between the two camps. We, too, can appreciate the wonderful home built by the deceased in a world devoid of decency and morality.

5. פ׳ חיי שרה: ḤAYEI SARAH

"And the life of Sarah was a hundred and seven and twenty years" (Genesis 23:1).
Our Sages commented that Sarah was as sinless at one hundred as she was at twenty, and as beautiful at twenty as she was at seven. Such a woman is seldom found.

* * * * *

"And Abraham came to mourn for Sarah" (Genesis 23:2).
Our Sages observed: "Whence did he come? From Mt. Moriah."
The finest eulogy Abraham could offer was a tribute to Sarah for
having reared a son who would gladly give his life for God.

6. פ׳ תולדות: TOLEDOT

"And Jacob sod pottage" (Genesis 25:29).
Our Sages discerned that Jacob was mourning for his grandfather
Abraham and busied himself preparing the mourner's meal of
lentils. Not so Esau, who was not moved by the loss of his grandfather.

7. פ׳ ויצא: VAYEITZEI

"And Jacob went out from Beer-sheba" (Genesis 28:10).
The departure of a righteous person leaves a painful vacuum.

8. פ׳ וישלח: VAYISHLAḤ

"Thy name shall be called no more Jacob, but Israel" (Genesis
32:29).
Israel was the name Jacob earned after wrestling with the Angel.
The deceased was the Israel of our "neighborhood."

9. פ׳ וישב: VAYEISHEV

"But he refused to be comforted" (Genesis 37:35).
Rashi adds that one does not find comfort concerning a *living*
person. The physical death of a loved one can, with time, be
accepted with a sense of resignation. David expressed this
thought when his baby boy died: "I shall go to him, but he will
not return to me" (II Samuel 12:23), because he believed that the
spirit lives on even in death. However, for a *spiritual* death there
is no consolation.

10. פ׳ מקץ: MIKEITZ

"And Joseph was the governor over the land" (Genesis 42:6).
According to tradition, Joseph provided *spiritual* food for those
who were hungry for the word of God.

11. פ׳ ויגש: VAYIGASH

"Also regard not your stuff" (Genesis 45:20).
All material things one values during his lifetime become worth-
less when he is about to leave this world.

12. פ׳ ויחי: VAYEHI

"Rachel died unto me" (Genesis 48:7).
Rachel, his beloved, died *unto him* alone. The pain of bereavement is most excruciating for the surviving spouse.

*　*　*　*　*

"And when Jacob made an end of charging his sons, he gathered
up his feet into the bed and expired" (Genesis 49:33).
Blessed is the parent who can speak to his children before he
passes on. His voice will be enshrined in their hearts forever.

שמות — EXODUS

1. ‏פ׳ שמות‎: SHEMOT

"When ye go, ye shall not go empty" (Exodus 3:21).
This is an imperative message for everyone: When you go to the next world, you shall not go empty-handed, but will take along all the good deeds you have performed in this world.

2. ‏פ׳ וארא‎: VAEIRA

"As soon as I am gone out of the city, I will spread forth my hands unto the Lord" (Exodus 9:29).
The noise of the "secular city" is not conducive to high moral attainments, spiritual elevation or religious meditation. The deceased was a rare exception in that he stretched out his hands to the poor and in behalf of synagogue, Israel and all worthy causes at all times and in all places—in the countryside as well as in the noisy "secular city."

3. ‏פ׳ בא‎: BO

"For there was not a house where there was not one dead" (Exodus 12:30).
The passing of the deceased touched every home in town as if it were a personal loss for everyone.

* * * * *

"This month shall be unto you the beginning (*Rosh*) of months" (Exodus 12:2).
Rosh has a dual meaning: head (or beginning) and bitter herb. This has been a very bitter month for the mourners; the head of the family is gone.

4. פ׳ בשלח: BESHALAḤ

"And the Angel of God, who went before the camp of Israel, removed and went behind them" (Exodus 14:19).
The deceased who always served in the forefront of the community and distinguished himself in leadership roles "removed and went behind them." His vision, wisdom and dedication to sacred causes will continue to inspire us retrospectively. He is not gone; his passing is but a change of position in the community, which his memory will continue to serve.

5. פ׳ יתרו: YITRO

The *Haftarah* begins: "In the year that King Uzziah died (Isaiah 6:1) . . . and the posts of the door were moved" (Ibid, 4).
The many institutions that benefitted from the charitableness of the deceased are now shaking at their foundations.

6. פ׳ משפטים: MISHPATIM

"Thou shalt take him from Mine Altar" (Exodus 21:14).
It can be said of the deceased that he was removed by fate from the altar of sacrificial Torah study and service to the community.

7. פ׳ תרומה: TERUMAH

"And thou shalt put into the ark the testimony which I shall give thee" (Exodus 25:16).
Placed in this ark or casket is not a lifeless body, but Tablets of the Law, a man whose life was dedicated to the study of Torah.

* * * * *

"And the middle bar in the midst of the boards, which shall pass through from end to end" (Exodus 26:28).
Parents are the *Briaḥ Hatikhon*, the middle bar that secures the walls of the home and unites the family. The demise of a father or mother is the loss of the unifying middle bar and the collapse of the home.

8. פ׳ תצוה: TETZAVEH

"And the sound thereof (*kolo*) shall be heard when he goeth in unto the holy place before the Lord, and when he cometh out, that he die not" (Exodus 28:35).

That voice (*kolo*) that was heard when he entered in the Sanctuary of life will not be silenced when he departs from it, "That he die not," but live on in the midst of those who loved him.

9. פ׳ כי תשא: KI TISA

"Thou sayest unto me: Bring up this people; and Thou hast not let me know whom Thou wilt send with me" (Exodus 33:12).

Moses requested that God appoint a worthy companion to serve as his model of righteousness. It takes one such model to raise the moral standards of an entire community. The passing of the deceased leaves us terribly bereaved because it removes from our midst such a precious individual, a model of perfection.

10. פ׳ ויקהל: VAYAKHEL

"And he made the laver of brass, and the base thereof of brass, of the mirrors of the serving women that did service at the door of the tent of meeting" (Exodus 38:8).

The mirrors that were the gifts of the women reflected more than superficial beauty. They symbolized feminine modesty and piety that especially endeared these women to God. The deceased was of this genre of women whom God gave a place of honor in the Sanctuary.

C. ויקרא — LEVITICUS

1. פ׳ ויקרא: VAYIKRA

"When any man of you (*mikem*) bringeth an offering unto the Lord" (Leviticus 1:2).
The noblest sacrifice is *mikem*, an offering of one's self. The deceased was a practitioner of *self*-sacrifice.

2. פ׳ צו: TZAV

"And carry forth the ashes without the camp to a clean place" (Leviticus 6:4).
We, too, are charged to carry forth the ashes of the offering "without the camp to a clean place," where the deceased will dwell in peace until the coming of the Messiah.

3. פ׳ שמיני: SHEMINI

"Let your brethren, the whole house of Israel, bewail the burning which the Lord hath kindled" (Leviticus 10:6).
The death of a young person is so terribly tragic that it touches "the whole house of Israel," not only the family of the deceased.

4. פ׳ תזריע: TAZRIA

"Then the priest shall pronounce him clean" (Leviticus 13:16).
The deceased spent a lifetime treating the moral plagues of society with love, kindness and an optimistic faith in the ethical perfectability of man.

5. פ׳ מצרע: METZORA

"Thus ye shall separate the Children of Israel from their uncleanness" (Leviticus 15:31).
The deceased loved his people and believed in the "Tabernacle

that is within them." Thus, he consecrated the best years of his life to the spiritual and ethical elevation of Israel.

6. פ׳ אחרי מות :AHAREI MOT

"And the Lord spoke unto Moses after the death of (*aharei mot*) the two sons of Aaron" (Leviticus 16:1).
What compounds the tragedy of loss is the family's utter frustration, fed by a gnawing suspicion that death marks the termination of life and the end of existence. It appears to be a *terminus ad quem*, the finality of which compounds the notion of man's pitiful finitude, robbing life of all purpose and significance. The Torah assures us that there is an *aharei mot*, "after the death," a life everlasting, full of retrospective meaning.

7. פ׳ קדושים :KEDOSHIM

"Ye shall be holy; for I the Lord your God am holy" (Leviticus 19:2).
Holiness is the antithesis of death. Holiness purifies while death defiles. Holiness is God's invitation to the genuine *imago dei*. By becoming holy, man becomes God-like, and beyond the reach of death.

8. פ׳ אמר :EMOR

"And when the sun is down, he shall be clean" (Leviticus 22:7).
At the dusk of a person's life we become painfully aware of his clean record and pure heart.

9. פ׳ בהר :BEHAR

"It shall be a jubilee year unto you; and ye shall return every man unto his possession" (Leviticus 25:10).
The end of a righteous life marks a genuine jubilee, for the deceased departs for his possession, the just and deserved reward for the many good deeds accomplished in a life well-lived.

10. פ׳ בחקתי: BEHUKOTAI

"And the trees of the field shall yield their fruit" (Leviticus 26:4).
Torat Kohanim (see *Rashi*, Ibid.) comments that these are the
barren trees that will one day bear fruit. The desolation experienced by a grieving family will one day yield to the growing
realization that the fallen tree left fruit and seeds. Thus the Sages
observed, concerning Jacob's immortality: "As his seed lives, so
does he."

D. בְּמִדְבַּר — NUMBERS

1. פ׳ במדבר: BEMIDBAR

"And the Levites shall keep the charge of the tabernacle of the testimony" (Numbers 1:53).

The Levites were especially charged with the transport of the Ark within which rested the second Tables of the Law side by side with the original broken tablets (symbolic of the shattered dream of mortal man), and journeyed by God's command. Adorning the Ark was the standard of love, the color of which was black like the standard of Issachar. (I.e., the casket covered with the traditional black cloth is like the Holy Ark that contained the broken tablets, and is dispatched on its journey to the Hereafter only by the will of God).

2. פ׳ נשא: NASO

"And he that presented his offering the first day was Naḥshon the son of Aminadab" (Numbers 7:12).

On that day, observes Rashi, ten crowns were taken.

Today, a crown was taken from our heads.

*   *   *   *   *

What distinguished Naḥshon was his unconditional faith in God. It was he who anticipated the Splitting of the Sea by leaping into it *before* the miracle had actually occurred.

3. פ׳ בהעלתך: BEHA'ALOTKHA

"When the ark set forward" (Numbers 10:35).

Two inverted letter *Nuns* bracket this dramatic passage concerning the migration of the Ark, indicating that it is misplaced in this section of the Torah. Another ark is about to begin its journey, this one containing the remains of the deceased whose death was so tragically premature. This ark, too, is out of place, for the deceased should have been allowed many more years with his loved ones whose affection for him is unequalled.

4. שלח ׳פ: SHELAH
"And see the land, what it is (*Mah hi*)" (Numbers 13:18).

The expression *Mah hi*, what it is, appears in Scripture three times. The first one to use this expression was Ephron the Hittite: "A piece of land worth four hundred shekels of silver, *what is that (mah hi)* betwixt me and thee?" (Genesis 23:15). King David also employs that idiom when he pleads with God to inform him about his length of days, *mah hi* (Psalms 39:5). There is a vast difference between Ephron's *Mah hi* and David's *Mah hi*. Ephron's *Mah hi* was rooted in shekels, real estate and crass materialism. David's *Mah hi* derived from a concern about life, values and faith. The deceased, too, faced mortality with David's faith and the spiritual *Mah hi* of the psalmist.

5. קרח ׳פ: KORAH

"And the earth (*vatekhas*) upon them, and they perished (*vayovdu*) from among the assembly" (Numbers 16:33).
For the wicked, *vatekhas aleihem ha'aretz*, once the earth covers their remains, *vayovdu mitokh hakahal*, they are lost to the congregation. However, the righteous remain forever *bitzror hahayim*, bound up with the living, inspiring and enriching a grateful community.

6. חקת ׳פ: HUKAT

"This is the law: when a man dieth in the tent" (Numbers 19:14). For the righteous, this world is merely a "tent," a temporary abode on the way to a better world. The wicked are trapped in their worldly materialism while a spriritual elevation awaits the pious.

7. ‏פ׳ בלק‎: BALAK

"Who hath counted the dust of Jacob" (Numbers 23:10).
From the dust of the grave can come purification and holiness, as in the case of Caleb who was saved from the error of his fellow scouts because he meditated at the tombs of the Patriarchs. Thus, we believe that the righteous are greater in death than in their life-time.

8. ‏פ׳ פנחס‎: PINḤAS

"And it shall be unto him, and to his seed after him, the covenant of an everlasting priesthood" (Numbers 25:13). A Pinḥas is lost, but the covenant continues with the children. Thus, the houses of priesthood and Levi are built on firm foundations provided by the founding fathers who dwell in the dust.

9. ‏פ׳ מטות‎: MATOT

"Thy servants will pass over, every man that is armed for war, before the Lord to battle" (Numbers 32:27).
The righteous cross their own Jordan Rivers to continue their love, concern and prayers for their dear ones.

10. ‏פ׳ מסעי‎: MASEI

"These are the stages" (Numbers 33:1).
For the believer, death is but a *stage* of life.

E. דברים — DEUTERONOMY

1. פ׳ דברים: DEVARIM

"Ye have dwelt long enough in this mountain; turn you, and take your journey" (Deuteronomy 1:6–7).

The righteous see the Evil Inclination (and the temptations of the world) as an insurmountable mountain that was vanquished only through assiduous struggle and dedicated effort (cf, *Sukkah*, 52a). The deceased belonged to the company of the righteous who conquered the mountain. Instead of allowing him to rest on his laurels at the peak, *Hashem* ordered him, as He did the Israelites of old: "Turn you, and take your journey!"

2. פ׳ ואתחנן: VAETḤANAN

"For thou shalt not go over this Jordan. But charge Joshua, and encourage him, and strengthen him" (Deuteronomy 3:28).

Many of us, like Moses, are not privileged to enjoy the fruits of selfless labors. The dreams of a lifetime are realized only through the attainments of the next generation. Like Moses, the deceased could see his "Promised Land" only from afar. And like Moses, his labors will find fulfillment in the works of a new generation, his children and those who have chosen to affiliate with his vision of a better community, a more viable congregation and a higher code of Torah ethics for all.

3. פ׳ עקב: EKEV

"Thou shalt be blessed above all (*mikol*) peoples" (Deuteronomy 7:14).

This passage can also be read:

"Thou shalt be blessed from (*mikol*), i.e., by all peoples."

The great accomplishment of the deceased was the acclaim and respect he won from *all* people, Jew and Gentile alike.

Indeed, he attained the highest degree of religious achievement, *Kiddush Hashem*, the sanctification and glorification of God in the general community for which he set a much admired example of moral excellence.

4. ראה פ׳: RE'EI

"And if the way be too long for thee, so that thou art not able to carry it, because the place is too far from thee, which the Lord thy God shall choose to set His name there . . . then thou shalt turn it (i.e., exchange it) into money, and bind up the money in thy hand" (Deuteronomy 14: 24–25).
"And they shall not appear before the Lord empty" (handed) (*Ibid.* 16:16).
When a person contemplates his mortal frailty and considers his ultimate end, the "place . . . which the Lord shall choose" is never "too far." Charitable deeds assume a reflexive predictability. However, "If the way be too long for thee, so thou art not able to carry" the accumulated mundane wealth, "thou shalt . . . bind up (*vetzara*) the money in thy hand," i.e., *vetzara*, you shall spiritualize the materialistic wealth, so that it nourishes you on the "long way," the final journey, so that you "shall not appear empty" (handed) before the Lord.

*   *   *   *   *

"Ye are children of the Lord your God: ye shall not cut yourselves" (*lo tithgodedu*) (Deuteronomy 14:1).
The Talmud interprets *lo tithgodedu* as "you shall not form separate sects" (Yebamoth 14a) for your Father in Heaven lives! When Esau said in his heart "Let the days of mourning for my father be at hand; then will I slay my brother Jacob" (Genesis 27:41), he was terribly mistaken, for our Heavenly Father lives and, as Malachi postulated,

> "Have we not all one father?
> Hath not one God created us?

Why do we deal treacherously every man against his brother,
profaning the covenant of our fathers?" (Malachi 2:10).
The deceased was a true "philanthropist," a lover of all God's
children, an avid advocate of the brotherhood of man, *because* he
believed faithfully in the Fatherhood of God.

5. פ׳ שופטים: SHOFETIM

"For is the tree of the field man?" (Deuteronomy 20:19).
Indeed, man has been likened to a tree, as some read the text, "For
man is the tree of the field." When the tree is rooted, it stands tall
and majestic and seems imperishable. The tree is evaluated in
terms of height and width and, especially, shade. In fact, the Talmud formulates calculations of a tree's dimensions on the basis of
its shadow (cf. Erubin 43b). However, the exact measure of a tree
cannot be obtained until it is felled and lies prostrate on the
ground. How symbolic of man's fate!
When man is "rooted" in life his shadows, i.e., his human frailties
and weaknesses stand out. However, when he falls, felled by the
ax of time, he is perceived in a more charitable frame, and his
positive characteristics become more apparent.

6. פ׳ כי תצא: KI TETZEI

"When thou beatest thine olive tree (*lo tefaer aharekha*); thou
shalt not go over the boughs again; it shall be for the stranger, for
the fatherless, and for the widow" (Deuteronomy 24:20).
The Talmud relates: "At his (Resh Lakish's) death he left a *kab*
(i.e., a small measure) of saffron, and he applied to himself the
verse, 'and they shall leave to others their substance'—*Psalms*
49:11" (Gittin 47a).
Lo tefaer ahareikha may be rendered: you shall not be distinguished or glorified afterwards, i.e., charity which is postponed
for posthumous distribution is a poor substitute for philanthropy
and kindness practiced throughout one's life. The deceased was
one of those genuinely charitable people who practiced *tzedakah*
during his very noble lifetime.

''Thou shalt surely restore to him the pledge when the sun goeth down (*kevo hashemesh*)'' (Deuteronomy 24:13).
All we have—life itself—is but a pledge from God that must be returned *kevo hashemesh*, at the sunset of life.

7. פ׳ כי תבא: KI TAVO

''Blessed shalt thou be when thou comest in, and blessed shalt thou be when thou goest out'' (Deuteronomy 28:6).
As the deceased was a blessing when he came into the world and a source of great blessing during his wonderful lifetime, so may he find blessing as he leaves this world and takes shelter under the wings of the *Shekhina*, the Divine Presence, in the Next World.

8. פ׳ נצבים: NITZAVIM

''It (i.e., the Torah) is not in heaven'' (Deuteronomy 30:12).
And the earth is equally bereft of Torah now since this great Torah scholar and teacher of Judaism has been taken from us.

* * * * *

''And it shall come to pass, when these things are come upon thee, the blessing *and* the curse, which I have set before thee'' (Deuteronomy 30:1).
A truly religious person perceives the commingling of curse and blessing throughout the course of life. It is the blessing *and* the curse that is man's greatest challenge! To detect a shade of curse in every blessing (e.g., corrupting wealth) *and* a bit of blessing in every curse (e.g., learning humility from failure) is the noblest insight to which one can aspire. Grief and growth go hand in hand. And to know that both are from God: ''*I* have set before thee.''

9. פ׳ וילך: VAYELEKH

''Take this book of the law (*Sefer Hatorah*) and put it by the side of the ark of the covenant of the Lord your God'' (Deuteronomy 31:26).

We, too, have placed a *Sefer Torah*, a decent human being who lived Torah, by the side of the Ark. The Talmud compares an *adam kasher shemet*, a decent person who passed away, to a *Sefer Torah* (Shabbat 105b).

10. פ׳ האזינו: HA'AZINU

"And He said: I will hide my face from them,
I will see what their end (*aharitam*) will be" (Deuteronomy 32:20).
Repentance, afflictions and death atone for a person's sins. However, the sins of *aharitam*, i.e., "others," namely sons and daughters, are a brutal disappointment. Like Reuben, the father may lament: "The child is not; and as for me, whither shall I go?" (Genesis 37:30)—echoing the anguished cry of all fathers of renegade children: "How can I go up and face my Father in heaven, having failed to secure my children for Him?"

11. פ׳ ברכה: BERAKHAH

"So Moses the servant of the Lord died" (Deuteronomy 34:5). The word "died" is not employed by Scripture with respect to David's demise because he left children who followed in his path. Not so Moses.

BOOK FIVE

YOUR BOOK

„ועתה כתבו לכם את השירה הזאת" (דברים לא:י"ט)
''Now therefore write ye this song for you . . .''
(Deuteronomy 31:19)

| _______________ | _______________ | _______________________________ |
| Date | Sidra | Name of Deceased |

A. Torah Proof Text

B. Rabbinic/Midrashic Text

C. Eulogette Outline/Summary

D. Focussed Application to Deceased

E. Conclusion

YOUR EULOGETTE OUTLINE FORM

_______________ _______________   _______________________
Date   Sidra   Name of Deceased

A. Torah Proof Text

B. Rabbinic/Midrashic Text

C. Eulogette Outline/Summary

D. Focussed Application to Deceased

E. Conclusion

_________________ _________________ _________________________________
   Date   Sidra   Name of Deceased

A. Torah Proof Text

B. Rabbinic/Midrashic Text

C. Eulogette Outline/Summary

D. Focussed Application to Deceased

E. Conclusion

YOUR EULOGETTE OUTLINE FORM

Date	Sidra	Name of Deceased

A. Torah Proof Text

B. Rabbinic/Midrashic Text

C. Eulogette Outline/Summary

D. Focussed Application to Deceased

E. Conclusion

_____________ _____________ _______________________________
Date   Sidra   Name of Deceased

A. Torah Proof Text

B. Rabbinic/Midrashic Text

C. Eulogette Outline/Summary

D. Focussed Application to Deceased

E. Conclusion

YOUR EULOGETTE OUTLINE FORM

_______________ _______________ ___________________________
Date   Sidra   Name of Deceased

A. Torah Proof Text

B. Rabbinic/Midrashic Text

C. Eulogette Outline/Summary

D. Focussed Application to Deceased

E. Conclusion

_____________ _____________ ___________________
Date   Sidra   Name of Deceased

A. Torah Proof Text

B. Rabbinic/Midrashic Text

C. Eulogette Outline/Summary

D. Focussed Application to Deceased

E. Conclusion

YOUR EULOGETTE OUTLINE FORM

_________________ _________________ ________________________________
Date   Sidra   Name of Deceased

A. Torah Proof Text

B. Rabbinic/Midrashic Text

C. Eulogette Outline/Summary

D. Focussed Application to Deceased

E. Conclusion

_____________ _____________ _________________
Date   Sidra   Name of Deceased

A. Torah Proof Text

B. Rabbinic/Midrashic Text

C. Eulogette Outline/Summary

D. Focussed Application to Deceased

E. Conclusion

YOUR EULOGETTE OUTLINE FORM

_______________ _______________ _______________________
   Date   Sidra   Name of Deceased

A. Torah Proof Text

B. Rabbinic/Midrashic Text

C. Eulogette Outline/Summary

D. Focussed Application to Deceased

E. Conclusion

A. What you like about this book:

B. What you dislike about this book:

C. Your suggestions to improve the next edition of this book:

— — — — — — — — — — — — — — — — — —

Please mail this page or a facsimile of it, with your contribution of
Eulogettes to the forthcoming volume of *EULOGETTES*,

    To:
    Victor M. Solomon, Ph.D.
    741 Dearborn Street
    Teaneck, N.J. 07666